GERARD MANLEY
HOPKINS

GERARD MANLEY HOPKINS

GERARD MANLEY HOPKINS

By G. F. LAHEY, *S.J.*

HASKELL HOUSE PUBLISHERS Ltd.
Publishers of Scarce Scholarly Books
NEW YORK, N. Y. 10012
1969

First Published 1930

HASKELL HOUSE PUBLISHERS Ltd.
Publishers of Scarce Scholarly Books
280 LAFAYETTE STREET
NEW YORK, N. Y. 10012

Library of Congress Catalog Card Number: 72-95435

Standard Book Number 8383-0986-0

To M. I.

PREFACE

THIS little study is an attempt to complement the interesting, though necessarily limited knowledge of Gerard Manley Hopkins derived from the reading of his poetical works. As the evolution of his character is peculiarly fascinating, I have included poems to show it, some of which artistically, are trivial and unconvincing, yet biographically are of extreme importance. Prose extracts have been printed as appendixes because their artistry is sometimes evanescent; it is, however, only by a sympathetic surrender to them that a reader will obtain that 'apperceptive' approach which is indispensable for a complete understanding of Hopkins's ideals. A chapter on his craftsmanship, in which the fundamentals of ordinary prosody are presupposed, has been inserted for those who are interested in Hopkins's system. There are several essays written for his Oxford tutors, as well as letters from Archbishop Walsh, Bishop Mandell Creighton, Sir John Rhŷs, Professor Skeat, Sir Robert Prescott Stewart, Mus. Doc., which have not been printed, for they are concerned with technical matters only, and, except for the names of their writers, would not interest any who will read this book.

Among many others, my thanks are especially due to Mr. Cyril Hopkins and Miss Kate Hopkins for their generous information about their brother's early life; to Mr. Gerard Hopkins for the early prize poems of his Uncle; to Dr. Bridges and the Oxford University Press for permission to reprint the letter from Hopkins to Dolben, and various poems; to Dr. Bridges and Mr. Murray for permission to reprint the letter from Hopkins to R. W. Dixon; to Mr. Basil Champneys and Messrs. Bell and Sons for permission to reprint Hopkins's letters to Patmore; to the Fathers of the Oratory for Hopkins's letters to Newman; to Father Keating, S.J., for Hopkins's diaries and correspondence without which this book would not have been possible.

CONTENTS

'The world shall glean of me—me the sleeper.'
FRANCIS THOMPSON

I

EARLY LIFE

GERARD MANLEY HOPKINS was born at Stratford, Essex, on 11 June 1844. The eldest child in a family of eight, he was a happy reincarnation of the many characteristics which gave to each of his parents a rare charm. His father, Manley Hopkins, was Consul General of the Hawaiian Islands to Great Britain, and combined a practical efficiency with a poet's vision. He was a clever man, publishing among other things a history of Hawaii: and many valuable works on marine insurance and cognate subjects. His love for the original and abstruse found an easy way into the mind of his son, as did also his poetic instinct, though his 'Spicilegium Poeticum' never rose to the heights of his son's poetry. Manley Hopkins's wife, the eldest daughter of Samuel Smith, a well-known medical practitioner of the early 'twenties in London, gave to her son her gentle nature and love for metaphysical speculation. She was an unusually well-educated woman for that generation, and her early acquaintance with German thought and literature, made her ever afterwards a keen student of philosophy, history, and politics. However, no one would have called her a Bluestocking —her habits were contemplative rather than apostolic. Her sisters, too, were talented, but as artists and musicians; and her brother's name still lives for his landscape paintings. This artistic strain in her family, and the poetical in her husband's, took deep root in the mind of their son.

B

When Gerard was but five or six years old, his character and education were being formed at home in a real, though unprofessional, way. A sister of his father was living with the family then, and being both a musician and a portrait painter, she found in Gerard an unusually promising pupil and accordingly coached the small boy in music and in drawing. His correct ear and clear, sweet voice made him an easy and graceful master of the traditional English, Jacobean, and Irish airs. This love for music never left him, and years afterwards, in the Society of Jesus, he used often to appear at their musical entertainments to sing, like .William Blake, the songs he had composed and put to music. All his life he was composing songs and .melodies, and until he studied musical theory under Dr. R. P. Stewart in Dublin, he used to bring them home for his sister, Grace, to harmonize for him. His early tutor discerned also a bent for painting in her nephew, and encouraged him in that direction. His success was so great that had his career not been shaped by other incidents he would undoubtedly have adopted painting for his profession, as a future drawing-master strongly advised him to do. This same aunt fed his eager imagination with the then recent discoveries of Layard so that her young pupil was continually drawing subjects suggested by them.

The precocity of the young boy must have been great, because his elders were more than a little alarmed at his youthful accomplishments. This alarm was not in the least dissipated by his own talk, since the originality in thought and word, which so distinguished him in later life, was very much in evidence even in his childhood. An inherent delicacy, which was far from mere fastidiousness, made him at all times over-sensitive to moral disorder and physical ugliness. His mother used to tell how, when he and his smaller brother were in the throes of an epidemic incident to childhood, she came into the nursery and found Gerard crying; on her asking the cause of his grief, he sobbed out: 'Because Cyril has become so ugly!' Later, in the slums of Liverpool and Dublin, the physical conditions of the poor distressed him much, and here again his compassion was stirred by the external disorder and ugliness.

In 1852, when he was just turning eight years of age, he had his first trip from home during his parents' removal from Stratford to Oak Hill, Hampstead. He and his younger brother were sent to relatives at Hainault Forest, where they spent their summer in the woods probing into the mysteries of nature. The incident is hardly worth recording except for the fact that it strengthened and improved his life-long delight in, and faithful recording of, what he saw in natural phenomena. In the autumn of that same year he was sent to a day-school in Hampstead, and two years later he was transferred to Sir Robert Cholmond-ley's Grammar School at Highgate, a place formerly associated with such illustrious names as Lamb, Keats, Coleridge, and De Quincey. Here Gerard made many friends, among whom was Ernest Hartley Coleridge, a grandson of the poet. Gerard visited the youthful Coleridge at his home, and met his parents and his sister, Christabel, who afterwards distinguished herself as a novelist. E. H. Coleridge himself became a well-known *littérateur*, famous for his life of Byron; and his youthful intercourse with Hopkins must have left its stamp on both. He always cherished his early friendship with Gerard, and named one of his sons after his friend.

Another friend was Marcus Clarke, who subsequently enjoyed such brilliant fame in Australian journalism and letters. Gerard met Clarke in 1855 in the Isle of Wight, not far from Farringford where Tennyson was, and about the time when Tennyson was just completing his first monodrama, 'Maud'. The two boys became fast friends, and a few months later Clarke was sent to the Highgate boarding-school to be a fellow-pupil of Gerard. In his memoir of Clarke, Mr. Hamilton Mackinnon has written:

Of his school-days little is known, save what can be gathered from a little note-book—a kind of diary kept by him at that period. According to this book, he seems to have had only two friends, with whom he was upon terms of great intimacy. They were brothers, Cyril and Gerard Hopkins, and they appear, judging from jottings and sketches of theirs in his scrap album, to have been talented both as versifiers and pen-and-ink sketchers. . . . Among other jottings to be found in this school record is one bearing the initials G. H. [Gerard Hopkins] and referring to one 'Marcus Scrivener' [a nickname invented by Gerard for Clarke] as a 'kaleidoscopic, parti-coloured, harlequinesque, thaumatropic being!'

Such a description, coming from the pen of a boy of twelve, makes us look rather at the writer than at

whom it was written. Clarke was always a great ad-
mirer of Gerard, and years afterwards he introduced
him into a highly fantastical story called *Holiday Peak
or Mount Might-ha-been*. He relates how, after a
stormy night-ride in the Australian bush, he came the
following morning upon an old house and saw a bright
crimson scarf trailing from a window:

> 'An artist lives there,' was my first thought, for
> nowhere in the world, save in the pictures of Prout,
> do we see bits of colour floating about in that
> fashion.
> 'Yes, you are right,' said a young man emerging
> from the well-dressed crowd, which throngs in
> spring the steps of the Academy.
> It was Gerard!
> Gerard, my boy-friend, who fled from Oxford to
> Stonyhurst, and embraced the discipline of Loyola.
> 'Gerard, what means this?'
> 'Dear old fellow!' said he, putting his arm round
> my neck, in the fond old schoolboy fashion, 'It
> means that I thought better of my resolve, and
> followed out the natural bent of my talents. My
> picture, the "Death of Alkibiades", is the talk of the
> year. I shall soon be as famous as you.'
> 'As I? You jest. . . .'
> 'Ah! lucky fellow!' said Gerard, 'how different
> things *might have been*. . . .'

This quotation has a triple interest. It is a proof of
the author's feeling for Gerard. It emphasizes the permanent effect of Hopkins's personality, for Marcus
Clarke had settled in Victoria quite ten years before it

was published; and they had never corresponded. Lastly, it illustrates the bent of Hopkins's talents at school.

Mr. Cyril Hopkins has recalled two incidents of Gerard's school life which will illustrate another phase of his youthful character:

> Of moral courage he had an ample supply. There was also a vein of eccentricity in his character which somewhat marred the beauty of it, and sometimes led him into difficulties that might easily have been avoided.
>
> One day he informed his friends at Elgin House [1] that, observing that nearly every one consumed more liquids than was good for them, he would prove the correctness of his theory by abstaining from drinking anything whatever for a week.
>
> And he carried out his resolution and could not be persuaded to desist until the period in question had gone by.
>
> The effect was that he collapsed when at drill, and had to ask leave to go home (i.e. to Elgin House), for the drilling took place in the playground. When informed, after he had left, of the cause of his indisposition, the old drill sergeant (an ex-Guardsman) thought it incredible, and could not believe it to be true. Upon which, the boy who had told him, and who was far from being sympathetic, exclaimed, 'A lie indeed! *He* tell a lie? Why, he would rather die!'
>
> And I well remember the astonishment depicted

---

[1] One of the 'Houses' of the boarding school.

on the old soldier's face and his outburst: 'If I'd only known it, I would have put his head under that pump!' pointing to the pump that stood in the playground.

On another occasion, Gerard discovered that every one ate too much salt at their meals, and passed a week without taking any, in the same manner. This latter experiment was not so trying as the other, but both required not only severe self-restraint, but much moral courage in facing hostile public opinion, which can make itself felt at a school as much or perhaps more than anywhere else.

It was at Highgate that Gerard came into contact with one who, in after life, was to become a very intimate friend. Richard Watson Dixon, poet, artist, and historian, had just taken his degree at Oxford, and had been ordained to a curacy in Lambeth. He taught some time at the Highgate School, and it was in him (though indeed the latter was unconscious of it at the time) that Gerard had found an object for his boyish reverence. Yet, strangely enough, it is improbable that they spoke much to each other. Dixon, however, always remembered him, and in a letter, 1878, he throws some light on Gerard as a boy:

I think that I remember you in the Highgate School. At least I remember a pale young boy, very light and active, with a very meditative and intellectual face, whose name . . . was yours. If I am not deceived that boy got a prize for English poetry!

This letter is interesting in the light of another comment of Gerard's brother:

> There is a passage in Lord Redesdale's *Memoirs* relating to the school-days of Swinburne, so suitable to those of my brother Gerard that I cannot resist quoting it:
>
> 'Of games he took no heed—they were not for his frail build; football and cricket were nothing to him. And so he led a sort of charmed life, dreaming and reading, and chewing the cud of his gleanings from the world-harvest of poetry, a fairy child in the midst of a commonplace, workaday world.'
>
> And like Swinburne, he was not deficient either in moral or in physical courage, for he was a fearless climber of trees, and would go up very high in the lofty elm tree, standing in our garden at Oak Hill, Hampstead, to the alarm of on-lookers like myself.[1]

The early poetry of Gerard is of extraordinary interest, and may be a pleasing as well as a valuable index to his early character. Like Blake he used to illuminate his manuscripts with his facile pen, externally embellishing what was of considerable internal value. One of his earliest poems, 'Spring and Death', is undated, but its form and content would suggest that he could not have been very old when he wrote it. He recounts, like the early medievalists, a dream,

---

[1] This is reminiscent of what Hopkins wrote in one of his diaries about ten years later: 'When you climbed to the top of the tree and came out, the sky looked as if you could touch it, and it was as if you were in a world made up of these three colours: the green of the leaves lit through by the sun, the blue of the sky, and the grey blaze of their upper sides against it.'

and his youthful reflections hover round the sad
transiency of beauty:

> . . . It seemed an evening in the Spring;
> —A little sickness in the air
> From too much fragrance everywhere:—
> As I walk'd a stilly wood,
> Sudden, Death before me stood:
> In a hollow lush and damp,
> He seemed a dismal murky stamp . . .

Then, after Death had marked the flowers and vanished:

> But the Spring-tide pass'd the same;
> Summer was as full of flame;
> Autumn-time no earlier came.
> And the flowers that he had tied,
> As I mark'd not always died
> Sooner than their mates; and yet
> Their fall was fuller of regret:
> It seem'd a hard and dismal thing,
> Death, to mark them in the Spring.

The poem reminds us somewhat of Moore, whose
songs and poems Gerard had known since he was five
years old. It led the way to a more ambitious attempt,
'The Escorial', written when he was fifteen years old
and which won the school prize that Dixon referred to.
The knowledge of art and architecture displayed therein shows us to what extent his early training had pro-
gressed. It is a poem of 135 lines, in Spenserian stanzas,
having for its motto:

βάτραχος δέ ποτ' ἀκρίδας ὥς τις ἐρίσδω.

The tenor of its lines manifests a knowledge of Byron
and at least an acquaintance with Tennyson. A few
stanzas will illustrate this:

> No finish'd proof was this of Gothic grace
> With flowery tracery engemming rays
> Of colour in high casements face to face;
> And foliaged crownals (pointing how the ways
> Of art best follow nature) in a maze
> Of finish'd diapers, that fills the eye
> And scarcely traces where one beauty strays
> And melts amid another; ciel'd on high
> With blazon'd groins, and crowned with hues of
>   majesty.
>
> This was no classic temple order'd round
> With massy pillars of the Doric mood
> Broad-fluted, nor with shafts acanthus-crown'd,
> Pourtray'd along the frieze with Titan's brood
> That battled Gods for heaven: brilliant-hued
> With golden fillets and rich blazonry,
> Wherein beneath the cornice, horsemen rode
> With form divine, a fiery chivalry—
> Triumph of airy grace and perfect harmony.
>
>   .   .   .   .   .   .
>
> The rang'd long corridors and cornic'd halls,
> And damasqu'd arms and foliag'd carving piled—
> With painting gleamed the rich pilaster'd walls—
> There play'd the virgin mother with her Child
> In some broad palmy mead, and saintly smiled,
> And held a cross of flowers in purple bloom;
> He, where the crownals droop'd, himself reviled

And bleeding saw.—There hung from room to
  room
The skill of dreamy Claude, and Titian's mellow
  gloom.

There in some darken'd landscape Paris fair
Stretches the envied fruit with fatal smile
To golden-girdled Cypris;—Ceres there
Roves through Sicilian pastures many a mile;
But, hapless youth, Antinous the while
Gazes aslant his shoulder, viewing nigh
Where Phoebus weeps for him whom Zephyr's guile
Chang'd to a flower; and there, with placid eye
Apollo views the smitten Python writhe and die.

In 1862 Gerard wrote a still more ambitious poem,
'A Vision of Mermaids', which also won for him
a school prize. It consists of 143 lines in heroic
measure. Its rich luxuriousness, unrestraint, and
wholly delightful fancy make it an extraordinary
achievement. Sometimes it breathes of Spenser, other
times of Keats. I quote passages of some length:

And it was at the setting of the day.
Plum-purple was the west; but spikes of light
Spear'd open lustrous gashes, crimson-white;
(Where the eye fix'd, fled the encrimsoning spot,
And, gathering, floated where the gaze was not;)
And through their parting lids there came and went
Keen glimpses of the inner firmament:
Fair beds they seem'd of water-lily flakes
Clustering entrancingly in beryl lakes:
Anon, across their swimming splendour strook,
An intense line of throbbing blood-light shook

A quivering pennon; then, for eye too keen,
Ebb'd back beneath its snowy lids unseen.
Now all things rosy turn'd: the west had grown
To an orb'd rose, which, by hot pantings blown
Apart, betwixt ten thousand petall'd lips
By interchange gasped splendour and eclipse.
The zenith melted to a rose of air;
The waves were rosy-lipp'd; the crimson glare
Shower'd the cliffs and every fret and spire
With garnet leaves and blooms of rosy-budded fire.

   .   .   .   .   .

This was their manner: one translucent crest
Of tremulous film, more subtle than the vest
Of dewy gorse blurr'd with the gossamer fine,
From crown to tail-fin floating, fringed the spine
Dropp'd o'er the brows like Hector's casque, and
    sway'd
In silken undulation, spurr'd and ray'd.
With spikéd quills all of intensest hue;
And was as though some sapphire molten-blue
Were veined and streak'd with dusk-deep lazuli,
Or tender pinks with bloody Tyrian dye.

   .   .   .   .   .

Soon—as when Summer of his sister Spring
Crushes and tears the rare enjewelling,
And boasting 'I have fairer things than these'
Plashes amidst the billowy apple-trees
His lusty hands, in gusts of scented wind
Swirling out bloom till all the air is blind
With rosy foam and pelting blossom and mists
Or driving vermeil-rain; and, as he lists,
The dainty onyx-coronals deflowers,

A glorious wanton; all the wrecks in showers
Crowd down upon a stream, and jostling thick
With bubbles bugle-eyed, struggle and stick
On tangled shoals that bar the brook—a crowd
Of filmy globes and rosy floating cloud:—
So those Mermaidens crowded to my rock.

    .   .   .   .   .

But most in a half-circle watch'd the sun;
And a sweet sadness dwelt on every one;
I knew not why,—but know that sadness dwells
On Mermaids—whether that they ring the knells
Of seamen whelmed in chasms of the mid-main,
As poets sing; or that it is a pain
To know the dusk depths of the ponderous sea,
The miles profound of solid green, and be
With loath'd cold fishes, far from man—or what;—
I know the sadness but the cause know not.
Then they, thus ranged, 'gan make full plaintively
A piteous Siren sweetness on the sea,
Withouten instrument, or conch, or bell,
Or stretch'd chords tuneable on turtle's shell;
Only with utterance of sweet breath they sung
An antique chaunt and in an unknown tongue.
Now melting upward through the sloping scale
Swell'd the sweet strain to a melodious wail;
Now ringing clarion-clear to whence it rose
Slumber'd at last in one sweet, deep, heart-broken
    close.

In 1857 Manley Hopkins with his two sons, Gerard
and Cyril, went on a tour through Belgium and the
Rhineland, providing Gerard with the occasion and

opportunity for more poetry and painting. In 1860 Gerard accompanied his father alone on a tour through southern Germany. He astonished his friends at home with a remarkable letter written from Nuremberg, and enclosing some first-rate sketches of Bavarian peasantry. Gerard made subsequent journeys to the Continent, one in 1868 to Switzerland, and one in 1883 to Holland, but the early travelling seems to have had the greater influence on his mind. Besides winning school prizes at Highgate, he won a scholarship, and in 1862 the whole course of his life was changed by his winning an exhibition for Balliol College, Oxford. He went up for the Christmas Term of 1863.

II

OXFORD COMPANIONS

Towery city and branchy between towers;
Cuckoo-echoing, bell-swarmed, lark-charmed, rook-racked,
   river-rounded.

G. M. H.

OXFORD, in the middle of the last century, was more than ever a theatre of great activity, and those who have studied the intellectual undercurrents of the period when Gerard Manley Hopkins was an undergraduate know how difficult it is to give it adequate portrayal in a short space. It will be remembered that the German Rationalism which seeped through the intellectual strata of England and Oxford in the days of, and partially on account of, Coleridge, and which rose to its greatest heights at the time of, say, Mill and his followers, was still in high flood; while as a bulwark against it were the various creeds of Christianity. Great protagonists of both sides said great things and excitement was high.

Hopkins came under the spell of many, among whom stands Jowett, not yet Master of Balliol and still fighting towards the guerdon of honour. He had already caused furore by his quasi-heretical, rationalistic editions of St. Paul in 1859, and his influence on the undergraduates was tremendous. Pater says that he was '. . . much read and pondered by the more intellectual sort of undergraduates', and Jowett himself admits that from 1860 to 1870 he was seeing every Balliol undergraduate every week! Walter Pater too, with his so-called daring philosophy and marvellous style, knew well the influence he exerted on the pupils who sat at his feet, of whom Gerard was not the least worthy. Then Henry Parry Liddon, who combined with his writings a most intense, loving, and lovable personality, famous in those days for his crowded Sunday evening divinity lectures, was Gerard's first confessor, and Gerard used to say that he never exceeded the contrition with which his 'first confession' was accompanied.

James Riddell, 'a most exquisite scholar', senior Proctor and select preacher in 1862 when Gerard came to Oxford, was his tutor and lectured to him on the *Odyssey*. Pusey knew the young man well.

Among his youthful friends, the names of Robert Bridges, William Addis, and Digby Dolben come first and easiest. Of Dr. Bridges we need say but little. A friendship begun in their early days at Oxford and continued throughout Hopkins's subsequent brief span of years brought them together much, and strengthened an ever-growing intimacy and understanding. The staunch love and the highest literary appreciation of him who was admittedly the best custodian of the poems, prevented Dr. Bridges from flooding an unappreciative and uncomprehending literary public with the rays of so original a source of pure poetry, so that he bided his time and with careful discrimination slowly educated his future readers with selections given to anthologies. After almost thirty years of patient waiting he published the slender volume of poems to which were added his own notes, the creative criticism of a delicate poetic sensibility.

The prefatory sonnet, written on the eve of publication, reminiscent, affectionate, loyal, may well find a place here:

> Our generation already is overpast,
> And thy lcv'd legacy, Gerard, hath lain
> Coy in my home; as once thy heart was fain
> Of shelter, when God's terror held thee fast
> In life's wild wood at Beauty and Sorrow aghast;
> Thy sainted sense trammel'd in ghostly pain,
> Thy rare ill-broker'd talent in disdain:
> Yet love of Christ will win man's love at last.
>
> Hell wars without; but, dear, the while my hands
> Gather'd thy book, I heard, this wintry day,
> Thy spirit thank me, in his young delight
> Stepping again upon the yellow sands.
> Go forth: amidst our chaffinch flock display
> Thy plumage of far wonder and heavenward flight!

Thus the knowledge of a friend combined with a rare faculty of criticism have fitted the Poet Laureate pre-eminently for the difficult task of editing the poems; and if occasionally he has prescinded from the well-spring of Hopkins's poetry—his religious ideals—or occasionally he has consciously taken exception to those lines which are so dear to Hopkins's 'co-religionists', his mind has been led into regions which, perhaps, are beyond the scope of any critic no matter how great. There may be disagreement with his comments on the 'Marianism' and 'ascetical' import of certain poems but it is intolerable that his understanding and sympathy for his friend should be questioned. Indeed one envies him his undergraduate days when in the flush and romanticism of youth he moved among his circle of friends who were so alive to the problems of the day. In his private diaries Gerard is constantly noting down appointments '. . . with Robert Bridges this afternoon. . .', while in the memoir of Digby Dolben, its author says:

> . . . in August . . . Gerard Hopkins came to me at Rochdale, and stayed, I think, some weeks. We read Herodotus together. He was so punctilious about the text, and so enjoyed loitering over the difficulties, that I foresaw that we should never get through, and broke off from him to go my own way. He had not read more than half the nine books when he went in for 'Greats'; this did not, however, prevent his success, and my tutor, Professor Wilson, who was one of the examiners, told me that 'for form' he was by far the best man in the first class. 'Form' was an all-pervading esoteric cliché of that hour. . . .

This literary friendship deepened with the passing years, ceasing at the poet's death only, and many of the autograph poems which carelessly left the poet's hands were carefully treasured by his friend, dating from 1867 to 1889.

William Addis was at that time even closer to Gerard in this coterie of friends, and years afterwards in the evening of life, when the former was beginning to see the harbour lights of eternity, he writes, reminiscently, 'with painful interest':

> Oxford, 5 July 1909.
> . . . I knew him in his undergraduate days far better than any one else did, and the feeling of initmacy on

his side never declined, until in 1888 I !eft the communion of the Roman Church. . . . Hopkins came
up from a High Church family. Both his parents
(whom I knew) were High Church of the Moderate
School. They were firmly attached to the Church
of England. . . . Of many letters some of them very
long which Hopkins wrote to me I have not, alas!
kept even one. We were almost of an age though
he was my junior in university standing. We walked
together almost daily, and when we left College
lived in the same lodging. He was at first a little
tinged with the liberalism prevalent among reading
men. I remember long arguments we had on the
eternity of punishment and in a walk on Headington
Hill he said, 'I never can believe that the Song of
Solomon is more than an ordinary love-song'. All
changed after his first confession to Liddon (that
kindest and best of men). Soon before his reception
by Newman he used to invoke the Saints and became
full of devotion to the Mother of Our Lord.
This would astonish me, for nobody else I knew
'went so far'. But he always had a fund of good
sense and modesty. He was far too real to indulge
in extravagant language. He could be firm and
honest though always tender and kind. George
Herbert was his strongest tie to the English Church.
. . . A thousand recollections crowd round me as
I write. Many a place here brings back the memories
of talks and disputes and happy affections in times
that now seem a long way off.

Yrs. faithfully,
W. E. ADDIS.

The diary, dated from 1863, is replete with observations of every kind, and a short quotation about a walk he had with Addis will illustrate the bent of his mind at the age of nineteen.

May 3. Walked with Addis to Stanton Harcourt. The Church is cruciform and rather large with a Norman door and several windows Early English... Pope finished his fifth volume of *Homer*, or the *Iliad*, in the octagon-roofed Kitchen, which, except one at Glastonbury is unparalleled in England.... Pope lived here two years, Gray, sometime... Charming place, rather my ideal, Stratford-on-Avon kind; willows, lovely elms; Pool and inky black water with leaves in it. Vertical shortish grass. Orchards with trunks and trees smeared over with the common white mixture whatever it is, rather pretty than otherwise. Primroses, large, in wet cool shady places. On the way, fields yellow with cowslip and dandelion. Found purple orchis which opens flowers from ground.... Crossed Isis at Skinner's Weir.... Beautiful effect with cloud. Wild apple beautiful in blossom. Caddis-flies on stones in clear stream, water snails and leeches. Round-looking glossy fieldmouse black.... Cuckoo-peewits wheeling and tumbling, just as they are said to do, as if with a broken wing. They pronounce peewit, pretty distinctly, sometimes querulously, with a slight metallic tone like a bat's cry....

Gerard Hopkins underwent not only much intellectual change and astringency during his undergraduate days, but also a religious upheaval so great as to alter entirely the future course of his life. It has, I think, been wrongly suggested that Jowett repelled the young undergraduate; indeed, on the contrary, evidence tends to show that it truly was the future Master who tinged this keen young mind with prevalent liberalism, and even as late as 1865, in a Platonic Dialogue on the Origin of Beauty, Gerard smiles almost irreligiously at the 'pomposity' of some of the constructions in the Prayer Book. That this religious aberration was neither of long duration or wide extent is clear from his other notes, although while confessing to Liddon as early as November 1864, he was still reading Jowett's *Epistles of St. Paul.* Ripples of the Tractarian Movement were still felt, Liddon and Pusey as its chief survivors were a real power in the land, but even they failed to satisfy entirely their protégé. Addis implies this when he describes a walking tour that he and Gerard took in the early summer of 1865.

Starting at Glastonbury and ending at Gloucester we did it by slow stages for he was far from robust. When at Hereford we walked out to the Benedictine Monastery at Belmont and had a long conversation with Canon Raynal, afterwards abbot. I think he made a great impression on both of us and I believe that from that time our faith in Anglicanism was really gone. He insisted that Anglican orders were at least of doubtful validity; that some grave and learned men questioned or denied their validity and that this being so, it was unlawful till the doubt was cleared by competent authority to accept

Anglican orders or even to participate in the Anglican Communion. So far as I knew, Father Raynal was the first priest whom Hopkins had ever spoken to.

The young men brooded long over their discovery and Gerard's diaries are filled with hundreds of lines of verse expressive of doubt, anxiety, fear, hope, most of which is too personal and introspective to appeal. He was now confessing to Dr. Pusey, and his confessions, it would seem from his other notes, verge on scrupulosity. His sensitive soul, naturally deeply religious, spent itself also in various acts of self-denial; for example he writes in Lent 1866:

> No pudding on Sundays. No tea except to keep one awake and then without sugar. Meat only once a day. No verses in Passion Week or on Fridays. No lunch or meat on Fridays. Not to sit in armchair except I can work in no other way. Ash Wednesday and Good Friday bread and water. . . .

This voluntary ascesis was practised the previous Lent, 1865, as is evinced by notes and sonnets; out of many I select the opening lines from 'Easter Communion' which seem to properly suggest the spirit of the rest:

> Pure fasted faces draw into this feast
> God comes all sweetness to your Lenten lips, &c.

One of his poems, written during the Lent of 1866, has never yet been published, and it is interesting not only from a literary point of view but also from a religious, being similar to Newman's famous poem antecedent to his conversion, which Gerard had previously transcribed into his diary:

Nondum

Verily Thou art a God that hidest Thyself.—*Is.* XLV. 15.

God, though to Thee our Psalm we raise
No answering voice comes from the skies;
To Thee the trembling sinner prays
But no forgiving voice replies;
Our prayer seems lost in desert ways,
Our hymn in the vast silence dies.

We see the glories of the earth
But not the hand that wrought them all:
Night to a myriad worlds gives birth,
Yet like a lighted empty hall
Where stands no host at door or hearth
Vacant creation's lamps appal.

We guess; we clothe Thee, unseen King,
With attributes we deem are meet;
Each in his own imagining
Sets up a shadow in Thy Seat;
Yet know not how our gifts to bring,
Where seek Thee with unsandalled feet.

And still th' unbroken silence broods
While ages and while aeons run,
As cast upon chaotic floods
The spirit hovered ere the sun
Had called the Seasons' changeful moods
And life's first germs from death had won.

And still th' abysses infinite
Surround the peak from which we gaze.
Deep calls to deep, and blackest night
Giddies the soul with blinding daze
That dares to cast its searching sight
On beings dread and vacant maze.

And Thou art silent, whilst Thy world
Contends about its many creeds
And hosts confront with flags unfurled
And zeal is flushed and pity bleeds
And truth is heard, with tears impearled,
A moaning voice among the reeds.

My hands upon my lips I lay;
The breast's desponding sob I quell;
I move along life's tomb-decked way
And listen to the passing bell
Summoning man from speechless day
To death's more silent, darker spell.

Oh! till Thou givest that sense beyond,
To shew Thee that Thou art, and near,
Let patience with her chastening wand
Dispel the doubt and dry the tear;
And lead me child-like by the hand
If still in darkness not in fear.

Speak! Whisper to my watching heart
One word—as when a mother speaks
Soft, when she sees her infant start,
Till dimpled joy steals o'er its cheeks.
Then, to behold Thee as Thou art
I'll wait till morn eternal breaks.

The poem clearly is one in which neither the poet nor the religious had found himself, but the hidden fire is there, and the nobility of 'golden youth'. It shows a spirit distressed and seeking, but in the night there were occasional peaceful moments of quiet wistfulness; a few months before this he had written his 'Heaven-haven', a poem in the diary originally of seven quatrains, though ultimately abridged to two and quoted by Bridges as such—its delicacy suggests, and almost surpasses, Tennyson, even at his best:

> I have desired to go
> Where springs not fail,
> To fields where flies no sharp and sided hail
> And a few lilies blow.
>
> And I have asked to be
> Where no storms come,
> Where the green swell is in the havens dumb,
> And out of the swing of the sea.

It seems almost superfluous to point out that many of the poems quoted here would probably have been suppressed by Hopkins had he foreseen the possibility of their publication. But, since they illustrate the growth of the man, to suppress them would be both a grave injustice to him and a violation of the canons of biographical delicacy and truth. The following poem is an extremely blithesome lyric, almost Jacobean in style and spirit, written in 1866. It is interesting to compare it with George Herbert's 'Easter' written in 1630, beginning:

Rise, Heart! thy Lord is risen. Sing His praise
                    Without delays
Who takes thee by the hand, that thou like-wise
                    With Him may'st rise—
That, as His death calcined thee to dust,
His life may make thee gold, and much more just.

Indeed the earlier poem is eclipsed in the expression
of the spontaneous joy of Eastertide since it is burdened
with an excess of the 'metaphysical' manner rather im-
perfectly used by the followers of Donne.

Easter

Break the box and shed the nard;
Stop not now to count the cost;
Hither bring pearl, opal, sard;
Reck not what the poor have lost;
Upon Christ throw all away:
Know ye, this is Easter Day.

Build His Church and deck His shrine,
Empty though it be on earth;
Ye have kept your choicest wine—
Let it flow for heavenly mirth;
Pluck the harp and breathe the horn:
Know ye not 'tis Easter morn?

Gather gladness from the skies;
Take a lesson from the ground;
Flowers do ope their heavenward eyes
And a Spring-time joy have found;
Earth throws Winter's robes away,
Decks herself for Easter Day.

Beauty now for ashes wear,
Perfumes for the garb of woe;
Chaplets for dishevelled hair,
Dances for sad footsteps slow;
Open wide your hearts that they
Let in joy this Easter Day.

Seek God's house in happy throng;
Crowded let His table be;
Mingle praises, prayer, and song,
Singing to the Trinity.
Henceforth let your souls alway,
Make each morn an Easter Day.

In the meanwhile Digby Dolben and Gerard Hopkins had met for the first and only time. Dolben was one of those spirits who are not content even with 'hitching their waggons to a star', but that needs must also 'scale the sky'. He had a mind no less penetrating than his friend's, and a soul equally sensitive to the seductive glow of nature and of art. Born at Guernsey on 8 February 1848, he spent his early youth at Eton, a friend of Bridges, and a hero-worshipper of Manning.[1] His personality was intense and affectionate, but buoyant and romantic; it is not surprising therefore, to find him surreptitiously visiting the Anglican Priory at Ascot, 'a Lodge of Jesuits at Old Windsor', a Roman Catholic priest at Slough, and returning to plague the Eton lecturer on religion with questions as distressing as they were fundamental. Being detected by his tutor in a stolen visit to the Jesuits, for his folly he was asked

[1] Manning was not the Cardinal, but a common friend of Bridges and Dolben, to whom the latter addressed many poems.

to leave Eton at Election time in 1863, returning again, however, having promised to guard his impetuous 'frailty' in religious matters.[1] He became an ardent Puseyite, and finally, under the name of Brother Dominic O.S.B. III, joined a third order of St. Benedict (Protestant) organized by the Rev. Joseph Leycester Lyne.

His poetry, if it has not the conscious power of the trained scholar, has at least the nobility and generous emotion of youth, being remarkable mainly in combining such intimate sympathy for the sensuous beauty of Greece with such profound love for the adorable beauty of Our Lord.

On 2 February 1865 he wrote to Bridges that he was coming to Oxford, and then it was that he met Gerard. 'It was at this visit, and only then, that he met Gerard Hopkins: but he must have been a good deal with him, for Gerard conceived a high admiration for him, and always spoke of him afterwards with great affection.'[2] How far this affection was reciprocated is difficult to say for Gerard wrote a few months later: 'I have written letters without end to the latter without a whiff of answer'. However, they did recover the threads of friendship, and Gerard followed his friend's enthusiastic loyalty in the pursuit of truth, with unabating interest. In September of 1866 just after he had seen Newman for the first time, he wrote: 'Walford believed that Dolben had been mobbed in Birmingham. He went in his habit without sandals barefoot. I do not know whether it is more funny or affecting to think of.'

[1] His father had remonstrated with him for his 'frailty' in this respect.
[2] *Memoir of Digby Dolben*, p. lxxii.

Poor Dolben was drowned in the following June while bathing in the river Welland, Gerard hearing of it only some weeks later. Dr. Bridges concludes his *Memoir of Dolben*[1] with an important letter from Gerard which, as it concerns both, we will quote in its entirety:

I heard of Dolben's death the day I returned from Paris by a letter from —— which had been waiting for me. . . . I have kept the beginning of a letter to you for a long time by me but to no purpose so far as being more ready to write goes. There is very little I have to say. I looked forward to meeting Dolben and his being a Catholic more than to anything. At the same time from never having met him but once I find it difficult to realize his death or feel as if it were anything to me. You know there can very seldom have happened the loss of so much beauty (in body and mind and life) and of the promise of still more as there has been in his case—seldom, I mean, in the whole world, for the conditions would not easily come together. At the same time he has gone on in a way which was wholly and unhappily irrational. I want to know whether his family think of gathering and publishing, or at least printing, his poetry. Perhaps you will like to hear what Dr. Newman says: 'Yes, we heard all about Dolben. The account was very pleasant. He had not given up the idea of being a Catholic, but he thought he had lived on excitement, and felt he must give himself time before he could know whether he was in earnest or not. This does not seem to me

[1] *Memoir of Dolben*, p. cxii.

a wrong frame of mind. He was up to his death careful in his devotional exercises. I never saw him.' Some day I hope to see Finedon and the place where he was drowned. Can you tell me where he was buried?—at Finedon was it not? If you have any letters from him will you let me see them some day? Among his poems is a translation from an epitaph which Chiabrera wrote for his own tomb in San Giacomo at Savona—Digby might have written it for his own restless, lonely, life:

> I, living, drew thee from the vale
> Parnassus' height to climb with me.
> I, dying, bid thee turn, and scale
> Alone the hill of Calvary.

Among Gerard's papers is a poem written before he entered the Society of Jesus, which may be an *in memoriam* for Digby Dolben. In the light of Hopkins's zeal for his friend's conversion there is an element of possibility in this view, but the tenor of the poem makes it less probable, and so I quote it here without further comment.

Remembrance and Expectation

> Soft and calm that pleasant eve,
> The closing of the summer's day
> When I sat dreaming there alone,
> Dreaming of the far away.
>
> Soft and quiet from blue to grey
> Changed the peaceful evening sky
> And swiftly as the flitting clouds
> My thoughts fled back to the long gone by.

Then spake my spirit: looking back
Hast thou not for which to grieve
And dost thou not at all complain
That he should die and thou should'st live?

And I made answer to my heart:
I cannot breathe one soft regret:
My faith is shining through my tears
That I shall see him—but not yet.

My dreams were of our holy love,
The sweet communion heart to heart.
We had bright hopes of earthly bliss.
And never dreamt that we must part.

We talked together speaking low,
We sat and sang together oft,
And side by side in church we knelt
And angels bore our prayers aloft.

And we were joyful, for the day
Was drawing near when it should be
That by His Priest God then should make
Us one for all eternity.

It came with its great joy, but 'ere
The sun had set that wondrous eve
I knew the story of my life
That he should die and I should live.

I did not cry aloud with pain
Nor plead with God, for I was blest,
And through my bitter tears I smiled
That he should go so soon to rest.

And thus I pondered wond'ring much
While I looked up with longing eyes
If my blue sky could be like his
There where he rests, in Paradise.

'Tis but a little while to moan,
'Tis but a little time to weep,
Till God shall say: It is enough
And then I too may fall asleep.

14 June 1868.

Such, then, was Gerard Hopkins during his under-graduate life at Oxford. Delicate of mind, cultured in many fields, it is of no small moment that he was a pupil of Jowett, Riddell, Pater; a disciple of Pusey and Liddon; a friend of Bridges and Dolben. Newman, too, enters largely into the story of his life, but this will be the subject of the next chapter. One has but to recall one's own adolescence—to pace round the haunts of one's childhood—to realize the import of so critical a time of passions and ideals, the re-shuffling of values, and appreciate how attractive is this period of Hopkins's life. Indeed, may one not say of it what Carlyle has said of another time and spirit: 'Those were great days, and to be alive then was very heaven!'

III

HOPKINS AND NEWMAN

THE more intimate letters of Gerard Hopkins would go far in establishing a deeper knowledge of his character, as they have done in other writers (notably in Charles Lamb) whose private lives have been far removed from the gaze of men. The defection may be adequately compensated by a study of the letters he himself received from his more intimate friends. It was a happy inconsistency in him who was so negligent about his own literary *arcana*, to have shown a practical orderliness in conserving so many of the letters that came to him, and it is our good fortune to possess the most important. In the following pages we will endeavour to present the effect on Hopkins of the overtures of some of the greatest minds of the nineteenth century and thereby gain a better knowledge of the atmosphere in which he moved.

At the end of August 1866, after returning home from a visit with Robert Bridges at Rochdale, Hopkins wrote the following letter to Newman:

REV. SIR,

I address you with great hesitation, knowing that you are in the midst of your own engagements and because you must be exposed to applications from all sides. I am anxious to become a Catholic, and I thought that you might possibly be able to see me for a short time when I pass through Birmingham in a few days, I believe on Friday. But I feel most

D

strongly the injustice of intruding on your engagements or convenience and therefore, if that is the
case, I shall think it a favour if you will kindly let me
know that you are unable to see me. I do not want
to be helped to any conclusions of belief, for I am
thankful to say my mind is made up, but the neces-
sity of becoming a Catholic (although I have long
foreseen where the only consistent position would
lie) coming on me suddenly has put me into painful
confusion of mind about my immediate duty in my
circumstances. I wished also to know what it would
be morally my duty to hold on certain formally open
points, because the same reasoning which makes the
Tractarian ground contradictory would almost lead
one also to shrink from what Mr. Oakley calls a
minimizing Catholicism. I say this much to take
from you any hesitation in not allowing me to come
to Birmingham if duties should stand in the way:
you will understand that by God's mercy I am clear
as to the sole authority of the Church of Rome.
While much in doubt therefore as to my right to
trouble you by this application, I would not deny
at the same time that I should feel it the greatest
privilege to see you. If it were so, I should hope not
to detain you long. I may perhaps in some way
introduce myself by reminding you of an intimate
college friend of mine, William Addis, who once
had the pleasure of spending an hour with you at the
Oratory; I think also he has written to you since.
I have little doubt that in not a very long time he
will become a Catholic. If I should be so happy as
to hear before Friday that you could spare time to

see me, I should hope to be at Birmingham that day
and sleep there, or if you had any convenient time in
the two or three weeks after that I should like to
come over from Rochdale where I shall be staying
at Dr. Molesworth's. But in ending I would again
say that I beg you will have no hesitation, as I have
no doubt you will not, in declining to see me if you
think best.

> Believe me, Reverend Sir, your obedient servant,
>> GERARD M. HOPKINS,
>> Oakhill, Hampstead, N.W.
>> 28 August 1866.

Newman replied, some weeks later:

>> The Oratory,
>> Birmingham,
>> 14 September 1866.

MY DEAR SIR,

I am sorry I was abroad when your letter came.
Now I am returned and expect to be here for some
weeks. I will gladly see you as you propose, if you
will fix a day.

> Very truly Yours,
>> JOHN H. NEWMAN.

G. M. Hopkins, Esq.

How many times in the next month they met, is
difficult to say, but Hopkins's letter of 15 October seems
to manifest a friendship deepened by acquaintance.

VERY REVEREND FATHER,

I have been up at Oxford just long enough to
have heard from my father and mother in return for
my letter announcing my conversion. Their answers

are terrible: I cannot read them twice. If you will pray for them and me just now I shall be deeply thankful. But what I am writing for is this—they urge me with the utmost entreaties to wait till I have taken my degree—more than half a year. Of course it is impossible, and since it is impossible to wait as long as they wish it seems to me useless to wait at all. Would you therefore wish me to come to Birmingham at once, on Thursday, Friday, or Saturday? You will understand why I have any hesitation at all, namely therefore if immediately after their letters urging a long delay I am received without any, it would be another blow, and look like intentional cruelty. I did not know till last night the rule about *communicatio in sacris*—at least as binding catechumens, but I now see the alternative thrown open, either to live without church and Sacraments, or else, in order to avoid the Catholic Church, to have to attend constantly the services of that very church. This brings the matter to an absurdity and makes me think that any delay, whatever relief it may bring to my parents, is impossible. I am asking you then whether I shall at all costs be received at once.

Strange to say, of four conversions mine is the earliest and yet my reception will be last. I think I said that my friend, William Garrett, was converted and received shortly after hearing of my conversion; just before Term began another friend, Alexander Wood, wrote to me in perplexity, and when I wrote back to his surprise telling him I was a convert he made up his own mind the next morning and is being received to-day: by a strange chance he met Addis in town, and Addis who had put off all thought of change for a year, was by God's mercy at once determined to see a priest and was received at Bayswater the same evening— Saturday. All our minds you see were ready to go at a touch and it cannot but be that the same is the case with many here.

Addis's loss will be a deep grief to Dr. Pusey I think: he has known him so long and stayed with him at Chale in a retreat.

I shall ask Father William Neville to open and answer this in your absence.

Monsignor Eyre seemed to say that I ought not to make my confession by means of a paper as I have been used to do. Will you kindly say whether you would prefer it so or not?

Believe me, dear Father, your affectionate son in Christ,

GERARD M. HOPKINS.
18, New Inn Hall Street, Oxford.
St. Theresa, 1866.

P.S. And if you should bid me be received at once will you kindly name the day? The liberality of the College authorities will throw no hindrance in the way.

At this time another character of great importance intervened in the path of Hopkins's choice in the person of Liddon, who hearing of his friend's intentions wrote four letters in rapid succession, and because they give a further insight into the two characters may not be

out of place here. They were written from Kensington
House, Brislington, Bristol, the first on 16 October:

> Coles has told me of the step which you are medi-
> tating. I do entreat you to pause. If I could at once
> see you, and talk matters over with you, as well as I
> can, I would; But I *cannot* return to Oxford until
> Monday. It must, I think, be plain to you that the
> Roman claims depend upon the truth of the
> Supremacy of the Pope, and that the supremacy (at
> least *this* is abundantly clear to me) is the upgrowth
> of times subsequent to the Nicene Council. The
> attempt to impose it upon the East was in fact the
> real cause of the great division of the church.
>
> From what Coles tells me I fear that you will
> consider my approaching the subject to you some-
> what in the light of an impertinence; and yet, after
> our intimate friendship with each other, I cannot
> bear to be silent, even though you should not be
> willing to listen. Perhaps I have inferred too much
> from his letter as to your state of mind: of course, I
> know that you have had anxieties on the subject
> heretofore, and are likely to be influenced by the
> example of friends whom you love. Let me entreat
> you once more *not* hastily to take a step which un-
> less it be certainly God's will, *must be* a most serious
> mistake.
>
> Ever affy.,
>
> H. P. LIDDON.

On 18 October, two days later, Liddon wrote again:

> I wrote to you a line two days ago, but am not at
> all sure whether I did not misdirect your letter. Its

purport was to *beg* you to hesitate before becoming a Roman Catholic. If you could examine your own thought fully, you would probably find that love and sympathy for Addis [1] is the strongest motive that is taking you to Rome. Such a feeling is natural enough towards such a man as he is: but in a matter of such vital importance, one clearly ought to act on nothing less than a strong personal conviction of being certainly right. Such a conviction could only legitimately be formed after a real examination of the points at issue, for which I am sure you will allow me to say, you have not yet had time. It seems to me to be clear that it is your duty not to act hastily in a matter where good men very deliberately take opposite sides, as if it were a question of obeying the first movement of the conscience in the way which is so necessary when moral evil is to be renounced. You will, I do trust, allow me to say this much to you—I cannot tell you how earnestly I trust that Our Lord will keep you from making a very serious mistake indeed.

On 19 October, the next day, Liddon again wrote:

I can hardly help hoping that you may have delayed taking the final and fatal step; and in this hope I write to beg you to consider the moral bearings of the line you have taken. Does it not seem to you morally certain that before consulting Dr. Newman or any clergyman of the Roman Church you ought, being placed in the English Church by the good Providence of God, to have seen what her clergy

[1] Addis had just previously been received into the church.

had to say in the way of relief to your difficulties?
You may say that you knew beforehand what English clergymen would urge; but, at least, *this* you
will admit that you were not likely, with your
studies lying as they necessarily do in quite another
direction, to be in possession of the English case,
except in a very partial and necessarily superficial
way. This being so, it seems quite clear that you
ought to have seen whether the particular difficulties which you tell me you wrote down on paper
could not be met. As it is, dear friend, what have
you done, but shut your eyes, and under the impression that you have had a call from heaven,
escaped from all further examination of the points
at issue? Of course the idea of the 'call' implies a
begging the whole question: it implies that you had
come to think yourself somehow in Ur of the
Chaldees, and likely to be denied to leave your
fathers' home for a distant Canaan.

On thinking this over I cannot altogether resign
the hope that you will see that you have acted
wrongly in neglecting the natural sources of advice
under difficulty, and in assuming too hastily that
you had had a special visitation of the grace of Our
Lord, with a purpose for which He could not be
supposed to vouchsafe one, except by a mind which
had already decided in favour of the claims of Rome.
Do have courage—to stop—even now.

Your father has written to me—of course in very
deep sorrow. I have replied to his letter, by saying
that I should hope to see you on my return to Oxford: I wish I could have told him that I thought

you would listen to what I have to urge. The moral
duty of delay appears to me so very plain, that you
will I hope and trust not have gone to Birmingham
to-day.

Forgive me for my importunity: but I cannot help
writing when so much of such vast importance to
you, is at stake.

Liddon's last letter was written the next day, on
20 October 1866:

Your second letter has just reached me. To set
myself right with you, I ought to say that I wrote
two letters to you before receiving your first. With
this you will, I suppose, receive one which I wrote
last evening, but which can scarcely go to Oxford
before this morning's mail.

As to what you urge about the manifest notes of
the church, superseding the need of historical and
other investigations, it is surely to be considered
that these 'notes' are not 'manifest'—in the sense of
proving the church of Rome to be alone the Catholic
church of Christ—since a large number of very
good and intelligent persons fail altogether to recognize them, and I do not think that a highly educated
man like yourself can safely suppose that the oppor-
tunities which God has given him can be set altogether aside on the ground that he is to 'find out
truth' by the same process as his uneducated
brother may who sweeps a crossing. Surely, e.g.
a mistake in your case would be a much more
serious matter.

Surely in order to be sure that you are doing

God's Will, so certainly, that you accept the responsibilities, so manifold and obvious—of your act with a good conscience, you ought to rest on something more solid than the precarious hypothesis of a personal illumination. Forgive me for what, God knows, I don't mean to be a sarcastic expression. But does not your account of what you are acting on in this grave matter, amount to this?

Nor can I think, much as I respect Dr. Newman, that he was the proper person for you to consult in your difficulty, or that his decision, as to the cogency or non-cogency of the reasons under which you are acting ought to have been accepted as final. Supposing that I were tempted to become a Deist, I should not go to Mr. F. Newman to ask him whether he considered my objections to the Catholic Creed sufficiently strong to warrant me in announcing my change of belief. I should, so to speak, give the system—if we must use that word for a part of the church of Christ—in which God has placed me —every chance of retaining my allegiance.

But you will have long ago been tired of my handwriting.

Yours ever affnly.,
H. P. LIDDON.

Such earnest and affectionate importunity from so great a champion of Christian dogma must indeed have caused his young friend pain; but it throws into greater relief the infinite gulf between supernatural faith and natural reason. They are in different orders of being. Hopkins realized that faith was purely a gift from God, which, once given, made any arguments from natural prudence or natural reason wholly superfluous. It would be like adducing syllogisms to prove to a man that he was in the full glare of the desert sun. An act of faith cannot be elicited by syllogisms (though these may help to dispose a man beforehand, and may strengthen him afterwards) for it depends ultimately on the mercy of God alone. Thus to Liddon, not having the gift of faith, such a request for further examination was eminently reasonable; but to Hopkins, once having received the gift of faith, any such procedure was unreasonable and even intolerable. So he went to Birmingham the following Sunday, and Newman's diary records simply: 'Oct. 21. Mr. Hopkins came from Oxford and was received.'

On that same day, Hopkins received a letter from Pusey at Christ Church whose disillusionment is numbed to indignation and verges on bitterness—perhaps each last member of the great Exodus silently rebuked Pusey's own *via media.* He had published the previous April his *Eirenicon* against the so-called extravagances current among Catholics, which he thought were barriers to reunion. He respected Hopkins greatly, and is said to have styled him 'The Star of Balliol', and so under this light the tone of his letter may be explained. He writes from Christ Church:

MY DEAR SIR,
I thank you for the personal kindness of your letter. It would not be accurate to say that I 'refused to see' you. What I declined doing was to see you

simply to 'satisfy relations'. I know too well what that means. It is simply to enable a pervert to say to his relations, 'I have seen Dr. Pusey, and he has failed to satisfy me'. Whereas they know very well that they meant not to be satisfied, that they came with a fixed purpose not to be satisfied. This is merely to waste my time, and create the impression that I have nothing to say. It has, in fact, when done, been a great abuse of the love which I have for all, especially the young.

I do not answer what you say in a note, because it would be still more useless. You have a heavy responsibility. Those who will gain by what you seem determined to do will be the unbelievers.

Yours faithfully,

E. B. PUSEY.

The wrench that the convert suffers can be known adequately by converts alone, and for Gerard Hopkins, filled as he was with such tender love for parents and friends, importuned by the intellectual aristocracy of Oxford, following the tenuous reasoning of his mind so subtly balanced and so analytic, that wrench must have been, naturally speaking, a martyrdom, compensated only by the inexpressible peace and exhilarating happiness that he afterwards experienced. Newman with his refined sensibilities and exquisite delicacy was indeed his ablest guide, and we find him writing to Gerard three days before his reception: 'It is not wonderful that you should not be able to take so great a step without trouble and pain . . . you have my best prayers that He who has begun the good work in you

may finish it—and I do not doubt He will.' Newman
writes on 21 November and again on 6 December
1866.

I am glad that you are on easier terms than you
expected with your friends at home. . . . I proposed
your coming here[1] because you could not go home
—but, if you can be at home with comfort, home is
the best place for you.

Do not suppose we shall not rejoice to see you
here, even if you can only come for Christmas Day.
. . . As to your retreat, I think we have misunder-
stood each other . . . it does not seem to me that
there is any hurry about it—your first duty is to
make a good class.[2] Show your friends at home that
your becoming a Catholic has not unsettled you in
the plain duty that lies before you. And, inde-
pendently of this, it seems to me a better thing not
to hurry decision on your vocation. Suffer yourself
to be led on by the Grace of God step by step.

In his next letter, 16 December, Newman again
presses Hopkins to visit him:

You are quite right to go home, since they wish
you, indeed, it would have been in every way a

---

[1] i.e. for Christmas vacations.
[2] There is an interesting story told which illustrates the different attitude
of Manning and Newman, both conscientious and far-seeing. An undergraduate of 1874 became a convert after his Moderations, wherein he
took a first class at New College. On consulting Cardinal Manning as
to his remaining at Oxford, the Cardinal was shocked and wondered if his
conversion were true—'Of course he could not', and he left without a
degree, a step which seriously hampered his career. Newman wrote to
Hopkins on 21 November 1866: '. . . I know you are reading hard but
give me a line now and then.'

pity, had you not resolved to do so. But I don't mean to let you off coming here. . . . Could you not come here for the week before term? I want to see you for the pleasure of seeing you—but, besides that, I think it good that a recent convert should pass some time in a religious house, to get into Catholic ways—though a week is not long enough for that purpose.

Newman writes about further arrangements on 14 January 1867, and Hopkins came the following Thursday. While there he met a Mr. Darnell, a former Fellow of New College, Oxford, and Anglican curate, who became a convert in 1847. At that time he was tutor to some half-dozen young men preparing for Oxford, and when Addis who was with him was leaving to become an Oratorian he was authorized to make the offer of his place to Hopkins. This explains Newman's letter of 22 February 1867:

> When you said you disliked schooling, I said not a word. Else I should have asked you to come here for the *very purpose* for which Mr. Darnell wishes for you. . . . I think you would get on with us, and that we should like you.
> Since then it was only delicacy which prevented my speaking when you were here, I have no hesitation in asking you to accept the invitation which we now make to you.

Hopkins took his degree in the spring of that year, and spent his summer vacation on the Continent, returning, however, to take up his duties at the Oratory on 17 September.[1] It was during Christmas vacation of that year that Newman wrote him about a retreat he was contemplating:

> It seems to me you had better go into Retreat at Easter, and bring the matter before the Priest who gives it to our boys. If you think that this is waiting too long, I must think of some other plan.

Why Hopkins did not return to the Oratory after the Vacation is not clear; but Newman writes again on 7 February apropos of his future state of life:

> You need not make up your mind till Easter comes, as we shall be able to manage matters whether you stay or we have the mishap to lose you.

Newman's next letter (14 May 1868) is to congratulate him on his chosen state of life:

> I am both surprised and glad at your news. . . . I think it is the very thing for you. You are quite out in thinking that when I offered you a 'home' here, I dreamed of your having a vocation for us. This I clearly saw you had *not*, from the moment you came to us. Don't call 'the Jesuit discipline hard': it will bring you to heaven. The Benedictines would not have suited you.
> We all congratulate you.
> Ever yours affectionately,
JOHN H. NEWMAN.

---

[1] Having taken a first class in 'Greats' at Oxford, G. M. H. naturally professed Latin and Greek. But he had from his earliest years a penchant for natural history, and this too entered into his classroom however unofficially; thus one of his former pupils tells me that he remembers him even catching frogs and newts for their lusty delectation!

Hopkins again spent his summer vacation abroad, and in the following September entered the Novitiate at Roehampton. Firmly established in his vocation, he no longer needed the advice of his great friend, and so their correspondence became naturally more infrequent, though indeed their mutual esteem and affection never lessened. Newman subsequently wrote to congratulate him when he took his vows and on the occasion of his Ordination, and also to reply to Hopkins's yearly birthday greetings. In these last, Newman often refers to the end of all his labours, as when he says in 1873: 'I am sure you said a good prayer for me upon it, for, at my age, it rather brings to mind one's death than one's birth.' In 1878 and 1879 Newman received his great academical and ecclesiastical distinctions—an honorary Fellowship at Trinity College, Oxford; and the Cardinalate—for both of which Hopkins wrote to congratulate him. Newman's answer to the former, dated 25 February 1878, contains the following interesting note:

> I am going to Oxford for a day to-morrow. I have not been there for thirty-two years, completed the day before yesterday. It is very kind of the Trinity men, but it is a trial.

In the spring of 1881 he wrote to Fr. Hopkins who was in the ministry at Liverpool and who had asked him about the respective merits of Carlyle and George Eliot:

> You are leading a most self-denying life, and must be heaping up merit. It shames one to think of it.

As to your implied question, I have read little of Carlile's [*sic*] and less of George Eliot, but I have ever greatly admired Carlisle's *French Revolution*, and, with you, think G.E., great as are her powers, nevertheless, over-rated. Perhaps, in number of pages, I have read much more of G.E. than of C., but one page of C. goes for many of G.E.

Two years later Hopkins pleased the Cardinal much by offering to re-edit his *Grammar of Assent* with a commentary and critical notes. It had been published in 1870; its originality and masterly psychology had received the serious approbation of competent scholars, but Newman with pleasing grace refused his offer.

Thank you very much for your remembrance of my birthday, and also for the complimentary proposal you make in behalf of my *Grammar of Assent*.

But I cannot accept it, because I do not feel the need of it, and I could not, as a matter of conscience, allow you to undertake a work which I could not but consider at once onerous and unnecessary. The book has succeeded in twelve years far more than I expected. It has received five full editions. It is being translated in India into some of the native tongues, broken into portions and commented on. It is frequently referred to in periodical home publications—only last Saturday week with considerable praise in the *Spectator*. Of course those who read only so much of it as they can reach while cutting open the leaves will make great mistakes about it, as Dr. Stanley has—but, if it is worth anything, it will survive paper-cutters, and if it is worthless, a comment, however brilliant, will not do more than gain for it a short galvanic life, which has no charms for me. Therefore, sensible as I am of your kindness, I will not accept it.

Hopkins replied that a compliment was far from his mind when he wrote, and hinted that England, like India, might welcome a comment, to which Newman again graciously replied:

In spite of your kind denial, I still do and must think that a comment is a compliment, and to say that a comment may be appended to my small book because one may be made on Aristotle, ought to make me blush purple! As to India, I suppose all English books, even *Goody Two Shoes*, are so unlike its literary atmosphere, that a comment is but one aspect of translation.

I must still say that you paid me a very kind compliment; you seem to think compliments must be insincere: is it so?

There remain a few letters written to Hopkins in Ireland, and of these, I select one, now famous, quoted by Ward, in his *Life of Newman:* [1]

Your letter is an appalling one—but not on that account untrustworthy. There is one consideration however which you omit. The Irish Patriots hold that they never have yielded themselves to the sway of England and therefore never have been under her laws, and never have been rebels.

[1] Vol. ii, p. 527.

This does not diminish the force of your picture, but it suggests that there is no help, no remedy. If I were an Irishman, I should be (in heart) a rebel. Moreover, to clench the difficulty the Irish character and tastes [are] very different from the English.

My fingers will not let me write more. [3 March 1887.]

There is a touch of real pathos in Newman's last letter to him on 24 February 1888, a lithographed acknowledgement signed with the wavering hand of an old man of eighty-seven. It was after this that Newman laid aside the mighty pen which had given so glorious a treasure to his Church, and to English Letters, an act which also closed a literary union and one of his most beautiful friendships. On the part of the younger man it must have been reminiscent of their initial separation, what Fr. Keating [1] has called: 'The spirit of sacrifice that could deliberately part fellowship with a man who must, one would have thought, have satisfied every exigency, intellectual and moral, of the young convert's being.' The sublime and lonely idealism which demanded the sundering of a cherished intimacy with the fine mind of Henry Parry Liddon, also severed a close companionship with John Henry Newman, but it brought Gerard Hopkins to a similar pinnacle where stood the older convert as the loftiest example of learning and holiness of nineteenth-century Catholicism.

[1] *The Month*, no. 541, p. 68.

IV

HOPKINS AND PATMORE

THE place that Gerard Hopkins holds in the economy of the spiritual and poetic life of Coventry Patmore is one of great importance. This throws a new light on their characters, and when we consider the wide circle of Patmore's friends supremely eminent in literature, politics, and religion, as well as the fact that Patmore and Hopkins met but twice during their short friendship of six years, it betrays a greatness in Hopkins's character which might otherwise lie hidden.

They met for the first time when Patmore visited Stonyhurst in the summer of 1883. His impressions were quickly formed, for a few months later he writes to Robert Bridges: 'I have seldom felt so much attracted towards any man as I have been towards him.' Six years later he again writes: [1]

I can well understand how terrible a loss you have suffered in the death of Gerard Hopkins—you who saw so much more of him than I did. I spent three days with him at Stonyhurst, and he stayed a week with me here; and that, with the exception of a somewhat abundant correspondence by letter, is all the communication I had with him; but this was enough to waken in me a reverence and affection, the like of which I have never felt for any other man but one. . . . Gerard Hopkins was the only ortho-

[1] *Coventry Patmore*, by Basil Champneys, vol. ii, pp. 6-55.

dox, and as far as I could see, saintly man in whom religion had absolutely no narrowing effect upon his general opinions and sympathies. A Catholic of the most scrupulous strictness, he could nevertheless see the Holy Spirit in all goodness, truth and beauty; and there was something in all his words and manners which were at once a rebuke and an attraction to all who could only aspire to be like him.

Patmore's first letter to Hopkins is dated 19 August 1883, and was written a few weeks after they had first met. With characteristic formality he addresses him 'Dear Sir', and though the later letters end with 'yours affectionately' yet never once does Patmore address the priest by any other title than 'Dear Mr. Hopkins'. There are twenty-nine extant and unpublished letters of Patmore to Hopkins, and it is reasonable to suppose that there were more, since the last was written more than a year before the latter's death and suggests no sudden cessation in correspondence. In the first he says:

Many thanks for your letter and the information about the poems. I shall send for 'Mano', and will be delighted to examine Bridges's verses. I quite agree with you about the archaisms which so many of our best living poets affect, and also, in the main, about rhymes. . . . What you say of 'Prometheus the Firegiver' makes me very anxious to see it. . . . If you could come and spend a night here I need not say that I should have the greatest pleasure in seeing you again.

On 18 September he writes to ask for Hopkins's

advice and criticism of his poems, which he is about to re-edit. Six days later he again writes:

> I am exceedingly grateful to you for the trouble you are taking in sending me most carefully considered notes and suggestions, with nearly all of which I agree, and mostly all of which I shall endeavour to adopt. . . . I cannot recover the mood in which I wrote, and were I to remodel a passage however short, I fear the alteration would look like a patch of a different colour. This may probably be my excuse for not acting on one or two of your strictures, though I think them quite right.

Patmore's next letter is also one of thanks, and on 31 October he again writes:

> Your careful and subtle fault-finding is the greatest praise my poetry has ever received. It makes me almost inclined to begin to sing again, after I thought I had given over.

It was not only his poetry but apparently also his prose that Patmore sent to his friend, for we read on 11 November 1883:

> I shall give your remarks on the metrical essay my best consideration together with the rules of the 'New Prosody' which Mr. Bridges has promised to explain to me, before I reprint the next edition . . . meantime I will only say that the substance of your very valuable notes will come in rather as a development than as a correction of the ideas which I have endeavoured—with too much brevity perhaps—to explain.

May I trespass still further on your kindness by asking you to glance over the inclosed verses of my son, who died lately, aged 22. . . .

Hopkins replied from Stonyhurst, 23 November:

In your son Henry you have lost a mind not only of wonderful promise but even of wonderful achievement. In the poems you have kindly lent me there may indeed be found some few immaturities, many expressions the echoes of yours and one or two perhaps of those of other poets, and the thought, both in its spontaneous play and also from the channel of reading and education it had of course run in, such as well to mark the writer for his father's son; still the general effect of their perusal is astonishment at a mind so mature, so masculine, so fresh, and so fastidiously independent: *sed erat,* as the Breviary says of St. Agnes, *senectus mentis immensa.* It is no disparagement to see in this (what I have seen in a remarkable degree in a young child) the unnatural maturity of consumption and the clear-sightedness of approaching death, forestalling by the refinement of the body what would otherwise have come with years.

What first strikes in the poems is the spontaneous thoughtfulness, the utter freedom from the poetical fashion and poetical cant of this age, and all that wilderness of words which one is lost in in every copy of magazine verses one comes across. Your example was however here a natural safeguard. The love of paradox, carried even to perversity, is due also to his birth or his breeding. The disdainful avoidance of affectation and vulgar effect leads sometimes to the ineffective, as in the last couplet of the line 'O for that afternoon': he would have come to feel this. To me the three most beautiful pieces seem to be the Sunset-poem, the lines on Flora's violin, and the Prologue.

But, if the poems have a shortcoming beyond points of detail, it would be in flow, in the poetical impetus, and also in richness of diction; they are strong where this age is weak—I mean Swinburne and the popular poets and, I may say, Tennyson himself—in thought and insight, but they are weak where the age is strong. He might have strengthened in this respect with growth, or have compensated for the want by weight and mastery of thought; but I have an impression that, had he lived, he would have laid his chief stress elsewhere than in poetry. Naturally, being who he was, to write poetry came to him first—his mind had been cradled in it; and even the metres he employs are those he was familiar with in you. But it seems to me, though it may look strained, that nowhere in these poems is there such a stroke of genius as the title of the piece on sunset. I should say he had, and would have found himself to have, a command of prose style by which he could have achieved more even than by that of poetry. The finest prose style is, in English at least, rarer, I should say, than the finest poetical. . . .'

So discriminating a letter warmed the heart of the older poet.—'I need not tell you how much delight

your opinion of my son's poems gives me'—so that
he dispatched two letters on 26 November, one to
describe his son's character, the other, a few hours
later, to thank Hopkins for praying for his soul.

On 9 December, Patmore again writes:

> I agree with almost all your criticisms on the
> 'Unknown Eros', but I fear that some of the most
> important cannot be acted on simply because they
> are so important. I don't feel up to anything much
> beyond merely verbal corrections. In my present
> state of poetical incapacity—which has lasted for
> two or three years, and may probably be permanent
> —I could only act on your very just objections by
> extinguishing the poems affected with the faults you
> point out, which I should be loth to do, though, of
> course, I would do so, if the balance of good seemed
> to require it. . . .

Of the Odes on Psyche which caused so much
discussion among Patmore's friends, dividing them
into two camps, Hopkins writes, 3 January 1884:

> . . . This poem and the two next are such a new
> thing and belong to such a new atmosphere that I
> feel it as dangerous to criticize them almost as the
> 'Canticles'. What I feel least at my ease about is a
> certain jesting humour, which does not seem to me
> quite to hit the mark in this profoundly delicate
> matter. . . . A single touch in such a matter may be
> 'by much too much'. I repeated to some one what
> I had read in the life of St. Theresa or Blessed Mar-
> garet Mary, that the saint had been at one time
> believed possessed, and was exorcised and drenched

with holy water: our Lord comforted her, telling
her that the exorcisms were not directed against him,
and could do her no harm, and that he liked holy
water. This, for a great familiarity, is credible. But
I heard my friend repeat it 'that he rather liked',
&c.—which is shocking. . . .

Patmore again agrees with the criticisms and replies
immediately elaborating the 'second coming of Our
Lord in ourselves in the flesh—that altogether marvellous and convincing sign, "sudden, surprising, un-
foreseen, immutable", destroying His enemies in us,
seizing and giving thousandfold life to them in us that
were alive; and raising many that were dead, and
dreamed not that they would ever be called upon to
give Him glory'. He concluded by saying: 'I shall not
consider myself "out of the running" so long as there
are a dozen men in England who think or speak of
the "Unknown Eros" as you do.'
It was on 28 January of that year that Patmore spoke
to Hopkins about the latter's poems:

Mr. Bridges and Mr. Gosse have excited much
desire in me to see some of your poems in manuscript.
I have felt somewhat shy of taking the liberty of asking you, but Mr. Bridges encourages me to hope
that you will not refuse my request.

In his next letter Patmore acknowledges the manuscripts and asks for a sufficiently long time to consider
the full import of Hopkins's theories as exemplified in the
poems. Hopkins who has been described as a 'poets'
poet', had received a comprehension of his theories

from Bridges and Dixon among his early friends, but from Patmore only uncomprehending astonishment. He writes to Bridges subsequently, confessing that he could not conceive how Hopkins's 'thoughts involuntary moved' in such numbers, and for him such poetry 'has the effect of veins of pure gold imbedded in masses of impracticable quartz'. Two weeks after Hopkins had sent him the poems, he wrote:

> I have read your poems—most of them several times—and find my first impressions confirmed with each reading. It seems to me that the thought and feeling of these poems, if expressed without any obscuring novelty of mode, are such as often to require the whole attention to apprehend and digest them; and are therefore of a kind to appeal only to the few. But to the already sufficiently arduous character of such poetry you seem to me to have added the difficulty of following *several* entirely novel and simultaneous experiments in versification and construction, together with an altogether unprecedented system of alliteration and compound words—any one of which novelties would be startling and productive of distraction from the poetic matter to be expressed.
>
> System and learned theory are manifest in all these experiments; but they seem to me to be *too* manifest. To me they often darken the thought and feeling which all arts and artifices of language should only illustrate: and I often find it as hard to follow you as I have found it to follow the darkest parts of Browning. . . . 'Thoughts that *involuntary* move

harmonious numbers' is, I suppose, the best definition of poetry that ever was spoken. Whenever
your thoughts forget your theories they do so move,
and no one who knows what poetry is can mistake
them for anything but poetry. 'The Blessed Virgin
compared to the Air we breathe' and a few other
pieces are exquisite to my mind, but, in these, you
have attained to move almost unconsciously in your
self-imposed shackles, and consequently the ear
follows you without much interruption from the
surprise of such novelties; and I can conceive that,
after a while, they would become additional delights.
But I do not think that I could ever become sufficiently accustomed to your favourite poem, 'The
Wreck of the Deutschland', to reconcile me to its
strangenesses. . . .

I do not see how I can say more without going
into the matter at very great length indeed; and, after
all, I might very likely be wrong, for I see that
Bridges goes along with you where I cannot, and
where I do not believe that I ever could; and I
deliberately recognize in the author of 'Prometheus'
a sounder and more delicate tact than my own. You
remember I only claimed to be a god among the
gallery gods. . . . Bridges's appreciation is a fact that
I cannot get over. I cannot understand his not seeing defects in your system which I seem to see so
clearly; and when I do not understand a man's
ignorance, I obey the Philosopher and think myself
ignorant of his understanding. So please do not
rely upon impressions which I distrust myself.

I should like to have the manuscript a little longer,

and shall be very glad if you will allow me to copy two or three small pieces for my own use. But I will not do this unless you tell me I may.

On 5 April Patmore received a letter from his friend explaining his method of writing, and he replies immediately for he had been 'feeling very anxious as to how you might have received my last'. He continues:

My difficulty in getting at anything very new is, as I have said before, greater than that of most persons; and sometimes that difficulty seems insuperable. It struck me, however, at once, on reading your poem, that the key to them might be supplied by your own reading of them; and I trust some day to have the benefit of that assistance. . . . The partiality and limitation of my appreciation of art often surprises myself. . . . Most of Beethoven, for example, seems to me to be simply noise; but when I do understand him, I understand him indeed. It was twenty years before I could learn to see anything in Wordsworth's sonnets to the River Duddon.

What you say concerning your modes of composition disposes, at once, of some of what I thought were sound critical objections against writing upon theory, &c., but *how* such modes, or at least some of them, as for example your alliteration, came to be the spontaneous expression of your poetical feelings, I cannot understand, and I do not think I ever shall. . . . I cannot help being a little amused by your claiming for your style the extreme of popular character. . . . Pray let me have one line some day to say that, however much you may despise me, you are not offended.

Such candour wedded to such disarming *naïveté* only endeared the older poet to the new, but, with the exception of three or four letters (in which they discuss Dixon's poetry and Bridges's easy profusion of 'highly finished verses') Hopkins's removal to assume his Fellowship at the Royal University with its consequent responsibilities, prevented much correspondence for the winter of that year.

On 4 April 1885 Hopkins breaks silence, writing from Dublin:

It is very long since I wrote to you: I now take the opportunity of holidays and wish you a very happy Easter. Some time back, I wrote you a longish letter, but repented of it, as I often do, and did not send it.

Part of it was to spur you on with your poem, and to that I return. You will never be younger: if not done soon it will never be done, to the end of eternity. Looking back afterwards you may indeed excuse yourself and see reasons why the work should not have been done—but it will not have been done: what might have been will not exist. This is an obvious and a homely thought, but it is a good one to dwell on. You wait for your thoughts voluntary to move harmonious numbers. That is nature's way; possibly (for I am not sure of it) the best for natural excellence; but this poem was to be an act of devotion, of religion: perhaps a strain against nature in the beginning will be the best prospered in the end.

You think, as I do, that our modern poets are too

voluminous: time will mend this, their volumes will sink. Yet, where there is high excellence in the work, labour in the execution, there volume, amount, quantity tells and helps to perpetuate all. If you wrote a considerable poem more it would not only add to your works and fame its own weight or its own buoyancy, but it would bulk out and buoy up all the rest. Are Virgil's *Georgics* and *Bucolics* read more or less for his having written the *Æneid*? Much more. So of Shakespeare's and Dante's sonnets. It was by providence designed for the education of the human race that great artists should leave works not only of great excellence but also in very considerable bulk. Moreover you say in one of your odes that the Blessed Virgin seems to relent and promise her help to you to write in her honour. If this is not to be followed, it is but a foolish, scandalous saying. You will not venture to say heaven failed to do its part, or expect others to say so; either then you deluded yourself with groundless hopes or else you did not take the pains of correspondence with heaven's offers. Either way the words would better have been left unsaid. This is presumptuous language on my part, yet aimed at the Blessed Virgin's honour, and at yours. . . .

Patmore's reply, dated 7 April, introduces a question which has caused much comment and of which we will presently treat; he says:

I was very glad indeed to see your handwriting again, and still better pleased to hear that there is a chance of seeing you this summer.

I believe that I have done all that it will be possible for me to do in the way of fulfilling the intention you speak of; but I do not think the work will ever take the form of a poem. I have written a series of notes which I propose shall be published after my death, under the title of 'Sponsa Dei'. I do not think they would be more, or so, impressive in verse. They lend themselves as little to verse as the *Epistles of St. Paul* would do—though there ends their likeness. I should much like you to read them, and hope that you will do so when I see you. . . .

The new edition of the 'Angel' comes out this or next month. I think I have adopted about two-thirds of your suggestions. I agree with all, but I have got too far away from my first feeling to dare any corrections which involve rewriting.

What you say about *bulk* in poetry being a good thing is quite true, I think; and I wish that I had force enough in me to make mine more bulky. But I have written all that I had to say, and as well as I could; and I must rest content. I spend many hours a day in meditating on my own line, but that line has carried me and daily carries me farther and farther away from the thoughts that can or ought to be spoken.

Let me hear from you as soon as there is any chance of my seeing you anywhere. If it can be *here*, you know how glad I shall be.

When the new edition of the 'Angel' reached Hopkins in Dublin he wrote, 14 May:

Thank you very much for the 'Angel in the

House', which reached me the night before last: to dip into it was like opening a basket of violets. To have criticized it looks now like meddling with the altar-vessels; yet they too are burnished with wash-leather.

In a letter of 17 May Patmore discusses the popularity of the poem in England and in America, and adds:

> A very good critic assures me that your suggested corrections have had a very decided effect on the impression made by the whole poem. It is wonderful how two or three awkward or unfinished lines deteriorate from a whole volume.

The next two letters are concerned with arranging a meeting, Patmore inviting Hopkins to Hastings, and offering, if necessary, to go to Hampstead to his home, or to Stonyhurst his head-quarters. In the first letter, Patmore suggests to Hopkins what he said so explicitly to Bridges four years later (already quoted), writing:

> I assure you that I shall always regard my having made your acquaintance as an important event of my life, and there are few things I desire more than a renewal of opportunity of personal intercourse with you.

Another invitation from Patmore on 30 July effected the meeting, and Hopkins visited Hastings during the early days of that August. It was then that Hopkins pronounced his fatal criticism of the now famous 'Sponsa Dei' about which so many have woven a tragic romance. It is probable that Katharine Tynan [1] has been guilty of an unconscious exaggeration when she wrote about it; and in the light of the various evidence and personal knowledge of Coventry Patmore's character, it is surprising to find Sir Edmund Gosse [2] placing the whole responsibility on the head of Gerard Hopkins. Dr. Garnett [3] implies that there were other influences at work and so does Mr. Champneys. [4] Patmore himself writes to Robert Bridges in the conclusion of a letter already quoted:

> The *authority* of his goodness was so great with me that I threw the manuscript of a little book—a sort of 'Religio Poetae'—into the fire, simply because, when he had read it, he said with a grave look, 'That's telling secrets'. This little book had been the work of ten years continual meditations, and could not have but made a greater effect than all the rest I have ever written; but his doubt was final with me.

Two years elapsed before he carried his decision into execution, for we find him writing to Hopkins, 10 February 1888:

> Much meditating on the effect which my manuscript 'Sponsa Dei' had upon you, when you read it while staying here, I concluded that I would not take the responsibility of being the first to expound the truths therein contained: so, on Xmas Day, I committed the work to the flames without reserve of a single paragraph.

[1] *Middle Years*, p. 349.   [2] *Coventry Patmore*, p. 169.
[3] *Dictionary of National Biography*.   [4] *Coventry Patmore*, p. 318.

That Hopkins did not intend the book to be destroyed seems clear from the following letter of 6 May [1888]:

Your news was that you had burnt the book called 'Sponsa Dei', and that on reflection upon remarks of mine. I wish I had been more guarded in making them. When we take a step like this we are forced to condemn ourselves: either our work should never have been done or never undone, and either way our time and toil are wasted—a sad thought, though the intention may at both times have been good. My objections were not final: they were but considerations (I forget now, with one exception, what they were): even if they were valid, still if you had kept to your custom of consulting your director, as you said you should, the book might have appeared with no change or with slight ones. But now regret is useless.

Patmore replied in a long letter, dated 11 May [1888] in which he says:

I did not burn 'Sponsa Dei' altogether without the further consultation you mentioned. After what you had said I talked with ——— about it, and he seemed to have no strong opinion one way or another, but said he thought that all the substance of the work was already published in my poems and in one or two of my papers in the *St. James's Gazette*. So I felt free to do what your condemnation of the little book inclined me to do.

In the light of these quotations, further comment on Gerard Hopkins's connexion with the 'Sponsa Dei' and the criticisms directed against it, seems unnecessary. The last extract is taken from the last-recorded letter of Patmore to Hopkins, and was written almost three years after the latter's visit to Hastings. During that intervening time their correspondence continued as usual, but where Patmore had hitherto ended his letters with 'Your very truly' he now writes 'Yours ever affectionately'; for the young priest gave much consolation and advice to him in his old age on matters literary, political, and religious. A few short quotations from Patmore's letters will illustrate this:

. . . [your visit] was a great pleasure, and much more, to me. . . .

I was very glad to see your handwriting again. Your letters are always very encouraging, and surely I sometimes require a little encouragement. . . . Your advice is excellent. . . .

Pray send me the 'long letter' when you find it, for your letters are quite events in my life of a hermit.

I am always raised in spirits by the sight of your handwriting, and I thank you much for sending me such full and lively letters in reply to my brief and dull ones.

Should your paper [on metre] be published I hope you will let me see it. I don't suppose that I have knowledge enough to understand all you have to say; but I may get glimpses.

Whenever I get a letter from you about anything I have written it makes me feel a little ashamed of myself; you give my words so much more attention

than it seems to me they deserve, and I feel that I
ought to have written so much better for such a
reader. . . .

From these and similar references in the letters
already quoted, it is possible to see yet another aspect
of Gerard Hopkins's character and genius, and it is
significant to note the respect, confidence, and admiration he evoked in other men whose names help to form
modern history.

V

HOPKINS AND PATMORE AND DIXON

GERARD HOPKINS's more intimate relations with Coventry Patmore have appeared in the shorter extracts of the last chapter. We will now conclude with three longer letters to Patmore, more general in tone, though valuable in content and association:

The Royal University of Ireland,

4 June 1886.

MY DEAR MR. PATMORE,

I have been meaning and meaning to write to you, to return the volume of Barnes's poems you lent me and for other reasons, and partly my approaching examination work restrained me, when last night there reached me from Bell's the beautiful new edition of your works. I call it beautiful and think it is the best form upon the whole for poetry and works of pure literature that I know of, and I thank you for your kindness in sending it. And I hope the bush or bottle may do what little in a bush or bottle lies to recommend the liquor to the born and the unborn. But how slowly does the fame of excellence spread! And crooked eclipses and other obscure causes fight against its rise and progress.

Your poems are a good deed done for the Catholic Church and another for England—for the British Empire, which now trembles in the balance, held in the hands of unwisdom. . . . What marked and striking excellence has England to show to make

her civilization attractive? Her literature is one of
her excellences and attractions and I believe that
criticism will tend to make this more and more felt;
but there must be more of that literature—a continued supply, and in quality excellent. This is why
I hold that fine works of art, and especially if like
yours, that are not only ideal in form but deal with
high matter as well, are really a great power in the
world, an element of strength even to an empire.

Believe me your sincere friend,

GERARD M. HOPKINS, S.J.

University College,
St. Stephen's Green,
Dublin.
20 October 1887.

MY DEAR MR. PATMORE,

. . . During the summer examinations, one of my
colleagues brought in one day a *St. James's Gazette*,
with a piece of criticism he said was a rare pleasure
to read. It proved to be a review by you of Colvin's
book on Keats. Still, enlightening as the review
was, I did not think it really just. You classed Keats
with the feminine geniuses among men; and you
would have it that he was not the likest, but rather
the unlikest of our poets to Shakespeare. His poems,
I know, are very sensuous—and indeed they are
sensual. This sensuality is their fault, but I do not
see that it makes them feminine. But at any rate
(and the second point includes the first) in this fault
he resembles, not differs from Shakespeare. For
Keats died very young, and we have only the work

of his first youth. Now, if we compare that with Shakespeare's early work, written at an age considerably more than Keats's, was it not? such as 'Venus and Adonis', and 'Lucrece', it is, as far as the work of two very original minds ever can be, greatly like in its virtues and its vices; more like, I do think, than that of any writer you could quote after the Elizabethan age, which is what the common opinion asserts. It may be that Keats was no dramatist (his 'Otho', I have not seen), but it is not for that, I think, that people have made the comparison. The 'Cap and Bells' is an unhappy performance, so bad that I could not get through it; senselessly planned to have no plan, and doomed to fail; but Keats would have found out that. He was young; his genius intense in its quality; his feeling for beauty, for perfection, intense; he had found his way right in his Odes; he would find his way right at last to the true functions of his mind. And he was at a great disadvantage in point of education, compared with Shakespeare. Their classical attainments may have been much of a muchness, but Shakespeare had the school of his age. It was the Renaissance: the ancient classics were deeply and enthusiastically studied, and influenced directly or indirectly all, and the new learning had entered into a fleeting but brilliant combination with the medieval tradition. All then used the same forms and keepings. But in Keats's time, and worst in England, there was no one school, but experiment, division, and uncertainty. He was one of the beginners of the Romantic movement, with the extravagance and ignorance of his youth. After all, is there anything in 'Endymion' worse than the passage in 'Romeo and Juliet' [1] about the County Paris as a book of love that must be bound and I can't tell what? It has some kind of fantastic beauty, like an arabesque, but in the main it is nonsense. And about the true masculine fibre in Keats's mind Matthew Arnold has written something good lately. . . .

Believe me very sincerely yours,
GERARD M. HOPKINS.
24 October 1887.

Milltown Park,
Milltown, Dublin.
6 May 1888.

MY DEAR MR. PATMORE,

. . . Since I last wrote, I have re-read Keats a little, and the force of your criticism on him has struck me more than it did. It is impossible not to feel with weariness how his verse is at every turn abandoning itself to an unmanly and enervating luxury. It appears too that he said something like 'O, for a life of impressions instead of thoughts!' It was, I suppose, the life he tried to lead. The impressions are not likely to have been all innocent, and they soon ceased in death. His contemporaries, as Wordsworth, Byron, Shelley, and even Leigh Hunt, right or wrong, still concerned themselves with great causes, as liberty and religion; but he lived in

[1] Act I, sc. iii.

mythology and fairyland, the life of a dreamer: nevertheless, I feel and see in him the beginnings of something opposite to this, of an interest in higher things, and of powerful and active thought. On this point you should, if possible, read what Matthew Arnold wrote. His mind had, as it seems to me, the distinctly masculine powers in abundance, his character the manly virtues; but, while he gave himself up to dreaming and self-indulgence, of course they were in abeyance. Nor do I mean that he would have turned to a life of virtue—only God can know that—but that his genius would have taken to an austerer utterance in art. Reason, thought, what he did not want to live by, would have asserted itself presently, and perhaps have been as much more powerful than that of his contemporaries as his sensibility or impressionableness, by which he did want to live, was keener and richer than theirs. His defects were due to youth—the self-indulgence of his youth, its ill-education, and also, as it seems to me, to its breadth and pregnancy, which, by virtue of a fine judgement already able to restrain but unable to direct, kept him from flinging himself blindly on the specious liberal stuff that crazed Shelley, and indeed, in their youth, Wordsworth and Coleridge. His mind played over life as a whole, so far as he, a boy, without (seemingly) a dramatic but still with a deeply observant turn, and also without any noble motive, felt at first-hand, impelling him to look below its surface, could at that time see it. He was, in my opinion, made to be a thinker, a critic, as much as a singer or artist of words. This can be

seen in certain reflective passages, as the opening
to 'Endymion', and others in his poems. These
passages are the thoughts of a mind very ill-
instructed and in opposition; keenly sensible of
wrongness in things established, but unprovided
with the principles to correct that by. Both his
principles of art and his practice were in many
things vicious, but he was correcting them, even
eagerly; for 'Lamia', one of his last works, shows a
deliberate change in manner from the style of
'Endymion', and in fact goes too far in change, and
sacrifices things that had better have been kept.
Of construction he knew nothing to the last: in this
same 'Lamia', he has a long introduction about
Mercury, who is only brought in to disenchant
Lamia, and ought not to have been employed, or
else ought to be employed again. The story has a
moral element or interest: Keats was aware of this,
and touches on it at times, but could make nothing
of it: in fact the situation at the end is that the sage
Apollonius does more harm than the witch herself
had done—kills the hero; and Keats does not see
that this implies one of two things, either some
lesson of the terrible malice of evil which, when it
is checked, drags down innocence in its own ruin,
or else the exposure of Pharisaic pretence in the
would-be moralist. But then if I could have said
this to Keats I feel sure he would have seen it. In
due time he would have seen these things himself.
Even when he is misconstructing one can remark
certain instinctive turns of construction in his style,
showing his latent power—for instance, the way the

vision is introduced in 'Isabella'. Far too much now
of Keats.

You sent me also a paper of yours in the *St.
James's.*[1] But I did not like the text of it, from Newman, and so I could not like the discourse grounded
on that. This was a paradox, that man is not a
rational or reasoning animal. The use of a paradox
is to awake the hearer's attention: then, when it has
served that end, if, as mostly happens, it is not only
unexpected but properly speaking untrue, it can be,
expressly or silently, waived or dropped. But this
you do not do with the paradox in question: you
appear to take it in earnest. I always felt that Newman made too much of that text: it is still worse that
you should build upon it. In what sense is man contemplative, or active, and not rational? In what
sense may man be said not to be rational, and it
might not as truly be said he was not active or was
not contemplative? He does not always reason;
neither does he always contemplate or always act—
of course human action—not merely go through
animal or vegetable functions. Every one sometimes
reasons; for every one arrived at the age of reason,
sometimes asks, Why, and sometimes says Because,
or Although. Now whenever we use one of these
three words we reason. Longer trains of reasoning
are rarer, because common life does not present the
need or opportunity for them; but as soon as the
matter requires them they are forthcoming. Nor
are blunders in reasoning any proof that man is not
a rational or reasoning being: rather the contrary:

[1] 'Real Apprehension', 20 January 1888. Republished in *Principle in Art.*

we are rational and reasoners by our false reasoning as we are moral agents by our sins. I cannot follow you in your passion for paradox: more than a little of it tortures.

Now, since writing the above, I have read the paper again; but indeed I cannot like it at all. The comment makes the text worse; for you say contemplation is in this age very rare indeed: is then reasoning in this age very rare indeed, or none? Other paradoxes follow; as that 'persons like General Gordon or Sir Thomas More would stare if you called anything they did or suffered by the name of sacrifice'. Did they then make no sacrifice? And if their modesty shrank from that word (I do not feel sure that it would) is the word not true? And do we not speak of Christ's sacrifice? and they were following Him.

Also the 'truly sensible man never opines', though 'many things may be dubious to him'. But the definition of opinion is belief accompanied by doubt—by fear of the opposite being true; for, since many things are likely only but not certain, he who feels them to be most likely true knows also that they may possibly be untrue, and that is to opine them—though in English the word *opine* is little used except jocularly. Here no doubt you did not want to speak with philosophic precision (and in the same way say that 'to see rightly is the first of human qualities': I suppose it is the rightness or clearness or clear-sightedness of the seeing that is the quality, for surely seeing is an act); but then the matter is philosophical: the title is so: the reference is to a philosophical work, and therefore philosophical precision would be in place, and I in reading crave for it. But you know best what comes home to the readers you are aiming at. Yet after all there is nothing like the plain truth: paradox persisted in is not the plain truth, and ought not to satisfy a reader. The conclusion about the unpardonable sin, is on dangerous ground; but I do not understand it, and few readers I think, will. You see, dear Mr. Patmore, that I am altogether discontented with this paper, and can do nothing but find fault.

And now, with kind regards to all your circle, I am, my dear Mr. Patmore, yours very sincerely,

GERARD M. HOPKINS.

Hopkins's friendship with Patmore is not unlike his friendship with another poet, Richard Watson Dixon. His name has already appeared in these pages. Living with Gerard Hopkins at Highgate, he spun the threads which were woven, long afterwards, into a friendship intimate and mutually beneficial. Eleven years Hopkins's senior, Dixon had been educated at Birmingham Grammar School under Dr. Gifford, and thence proceeded to Pembroke College, Oxford, where he moved in an exceedingly talented circle of friends. Like his lifelong friend Burne-Jones he painted, and with William Morris invented and projected the *Oxford and Cambridge Magazine*. Though he read Classics, yet his interests carried him far into the realm of literature and history, leaving to posterity several books of poetry and a better-known work on the Reformation in England. This last is one of the most authoritative publications of its kind and is distinguished for its impartiality, its profound research, and its extraordinary literary value. His poetry merits the distinction of being edited by the Laureate.

It was in 1878 that the acquaintance of Hopkins and Dixon was renewed. There are, at present, great numbers of Dixon's letters to Hopkins, acknowledging his valuable criticisms on Dixon's own poetry as well as on that of many of the major poets from Milton onwards. These letters are important only in illuminating further the character of Hopkins, and with this in view we will hazard a few selections. The following letter began their friendship:

Stonyhurst College,[1]
4 June 1878.

VERY REVEREND SIR,

I take a liberty as a stranger in addressing you, nevertheless I did once have some slight acquaintance with you. You will not remember me, but you will remember taking a mastership for some months at Highgate School . . . where I then was. When you went away you gave, as I recollect, a copy of your book *Christ's Company* to one of the masters. . . . By this means coming to know its name, I was curious to read it, which when I went to Oxford I did. At first I was surprised at it, then pleased, at last I became so fond of it that I made it, so far as that could be, a part of my own mind. I got your other volume, and your little prize-essay

---

[1] *Selected Poems of R. W. Dixon* (with a memoir), by Robert Bridges, p. xxxii.

too. I introduced your poems to my friends, and, if they did not share my own enthusiasm, made them at all events admire. And to show you how greatly I prized them, when I entered my present state of life, in which I knew I could have no books of my own. . . . I copied out 'St. Paul', 'St. John', 'Love's Consolation', and others from both volumes and kept them by me. What I am saying now I might it is true have written any time these many years back, but partly I hesitated, partly I was not sure you were yet living: lately, however, I saw in the *Athenaeum* a review of your historical work newly published, and since have made up my mind to write to you—which, to be sure is an impertinence if you think it so, but I seemed to owe you something, or a great deal, and then I knew what I should feel myself in your position if I had written and published works, the extreme beauty of which the author himself the most keenly feels, and they had fallen out of sight at once and have been (you will not mind my saying it, as it is, I suppose, plainly true) almost wholly unknown: then, I say, I should feel a certain comfort to be told they had been deeply appreciated by some one person, a stranger, at all events, and had not been published quite in vain. . . . Your poems have a medieval colouring like William Morris's and the Rossettis' and others, but none seemed to me to have it so unaffectedly. . . . I have said all this, and could, if there were any use, say more as a sort of duty of charity to make up, so far as one voice can do, for the disappointment you must, at least at times, I think, have felt over your rich and exquisite work almost thrown away. You will therefore feel no offence, though you may surprise, at my writing.

> I am, very Rev. Sir,
> Your obedient servant,
> GERARD M. HOPKINS, S.J.

The following letter from Dixon was written at Hayton Vicarage in reply:

REVEREND AND MOST DEAR SIR,

I received your letter two days ago, but have been unable to answer it before, chiefly through the many and various emotions which it has awakened within me. . . . You cannot but know that I must be deeply moved, nay shaken to the very centre, by such a letter as that which you have sent me: for which I thank you from my inmost heart. I place and value it among my best possessions. I can in truth hardly realize that what I have written, which has been generally, almost universally neglected, should have been so much valued and treasured. This is more than fame: and I may truly say that when I read your letter, and whenever I take it out of my pocket to look at it, I feel that I prefer to have been so known and prized by one, than to have had the ordinary appreciation of many. I was talking to my friend Burne-Jones the painter a while ago: about three weeks: who said among other things, 'One only works in reality for the one man who may rise to understand one, it may be ages hence'. I am happy in being understood in my lifetime. To think that you have revolved my words, so as to make them part of yourself, and have actually copied out some of them, being denied books, is to me indescribably affecting. . . .

I may just add that I received a letter of warm and high approbation and criticism from Rossetti (whom you mention in your letter) about three years ago, when he read my poems, which he had not seen before. Beside that letter I place yours.

But I am ashamed of writing so much of myself. . . . Let me regard with admiration the arduous and. self-denying career which is modestly indicated in your letter and signature: and which places you so much higher in 'Christ's Company', than I am.

In a second letter, 25 September, Dixon suggests the sudden and tremendous influence of Hopkins's personality over him.

. . . I feel ashamed when I look at your letter to see how long I have left it unanswered: and when I read it again, and consider the just and noble sentiments, the generous kindness, and the tender feeling which it breathes, I feel myself doubly criminal. But you must forgive me: for in part I feel personally unworthy to receive the admiration of such a soul as yours: and partly though I have often resolved to write, I have always found myself unequal to it, through emotion or darkness. . . . I have to thank you from the bottom of my heart for your letter; for the generous repetition of your opinion that I have been neglected, and your sympathy with the disappointment and pain, which you suppose, not unjustly, that I must have felt: but above all, for the passages in which you point me to Christ as the great critic, the unfailing judge of the gifts which He has given. I have drawn deep consolation from that: it came upon me with the force of a revelation.

In course of time, Hopkins sent many of his poems to Dixon, and the following letter will illustrate their effect upon him (26 October 1881):

> . . . I shall not attempt to thank you for your invaluable criticism. . . . But first, I hope that you are going on with poetry yourself: I can understand that your present position, seclusion, and exercises, would give to your writings a rare charm—they have done so in those that I have seen: something that I cannot describe, but know to myself by the inadequate word *terrible pathos*—something of what you call temper in poetry: a right temper which goes to the point of the terrible: the terrible crystal. Milton is the only one else who has anything like it, and he has it in a totally different way: he has it through indignation, through injured majesty, which is an inferior thing. . . .[1]

The following extract intimates the power of Hopkins's ideals (4 November 1881):

MY DEAR, DEAR FRIEND,

> Your letter touches and moves me more than I can say. I ought not in your present circumstances to tease you with the regret that much of it gives me: to hear of your having destroyed poems, and feeling that you have a vocation in comparison of which

[1] There is a postscript to this letter, of amusing poetic nonchalance: 'I ought to tell you that I am engaged to be married some time or other.'

poetry and the fame that might assuredly be yours
is nothing. I could say much, for my heart bleeds:
but I ought also to feel the same: and do not as I
ought, though I thought myself very indifferent as
to fame. So I will say nothing, but cling to the hope
that you will find it consistent with all that you have
undertaken to pursue poetry still, as occasion might
serve: and in doing so you may be sanctioned and
encouraged by the great Society to which you be-
long, which has given so many ornaments to literature. Surely one vocation cannot destroy another:
and such a Society as yours will not remain ignorant
that you have such gifts as have seldom been given
by God to man.

In another letter Dixon continues:

. . . This is intended not to be an answer to your
last immensely valuable letter: but an acknowledgement of the song which I have received. . . . I cannot
help, since I began this, taking up your last long
letter to read again. As to the first part of it, in
which you speak of your poetry, and its relation to
your profession, I cannot but take courage to hope
that the day will come, when so health-breathing
and purely powerful a faculty as you have been
gifted with may find its proper issue in the world.
B. struck the truth long ago when he said to me that
your poems more carried him out of himself than
those of any one. I have again and again felt the
same: and am certain that as a means of serving
religion you cannot have a more powerful instrument than your own verses. . . .

After much correspondence on the question the two friends eventually arranged a meeting, about which Dixon writes (13 April 1882):

> . . . how very glad I am to have seen you and to have a full knowledge of what you are like. So far as I can remember you are very like the boy of Highgate. . . . I feel the death of Rossetti most acutely. I have known him for twenty years: he was one of my dearest friends. . . . It leaves an awful blank. . . .

Hopkins was doing much research work for Dixon's *History*, on the Mission of the Society of Jesus in Ireland in 1530, and this was the subject of much correspondence. Dixon acknowledges his friend's help in a note in the *History*, and among other expressions of gratitude says in a letter (19 March 1885):

> I cannot say how much I thank you, or how valuable your help, or how I feel your goodness in bestowing so much labour. . . .

In 1881 Dixon had attempted to include some of Hopkins's sonnets in an anthology compiled by Mr. Hall Caine but nothing came of it. In 1886 he writes that he is

> employed by Messrs. Routledge the Publishers to edit a Bible Birthday Book: a collection of texts and verses of poetry. I want to include at least one of yours. . . .

This was more successful and several were printed.

The last recorded letter of Dixon to Hopkins was from Warkworth, 28 July 1886:

MY DEAR, DEAR FRIEND:

I cannot now answer your precious letter, but only thank you for it.

I have inserted your 'first fruits' piece, and propose, if you do not forbid, to put your name to it thus, G. (or else Gerard) Hopkins, S.J.

I have heard from Bridges to-day.

I dedicate to you my lyrical poems: but have not heard of them since I sent them to Daniel months ago. His health prevents, I fear, their immediate publication.

Your affectionate friend,

R. W. DIXON.

VI

THE CRAFTSMAN

FROM the first tentative appearance of Hopkins's poems in anthologies, the critical sensibilities of our finest scholars have ever been stirred. The impeccability of his craftsmanship often elicited unqualified and universal acclamation, the distinctiveness of his creative and synthetic originality left much for discussion. Never before, perhaps, has so slender a volume of poetry given such ample scope for so many diverse tastes and aptitudes.

Hopkins himself, in the crystallization of impalpable forms, realized the price his genius sometimes demanded from his craftsmanship. He wrote, in 1879:

> But as air, melody, is what strikes me most of all in music and design in painting, so design, pattern, or what I am in the habit of calling *inscape* is what I above all aim at in poetry. Now it is the virtue of design, pattern, or inscape to be distinctive, and it is the vice of distinctiveness to become queer. This vice I cannot have escaped. . . . Moreover the oddness may make them [i.e. the poems] repulsive at first, and yet Lang might have liked them on a second reading.

Every poetic distinctiveness has at first a certain obscurity, and any appreciation commensurate with poetic values will always postulate many 'second readings', much intellectual meditation—the 'salt of poetry'. Hopkins's oddness lies mainly in his verbal and rhythmic obscurity. But even this may please. His peculiar interest comes from the perennial source of surprises which meet any reader however well-informed; his peculiar greatness lies in the amazing union of intellectual profundity with great emotional intensity and imaginative power, under the control of a highly developed faculty of expression and structural perfection. It is well to remember, however, that these qualities may not be predicated indiscriminately to all his work. In fact before the 'Deutschland' in 1875 his poetry has but slight aesthetic interest other than youthful precocity and a certain idyllic sweetness. Later poems, such as 'Rosa Mystica' and 'Ad Mariam', are also of this category, though 'Rosa Mystica' has a simple beauty that would only be blemished by aesthetic self-consciousness. 'Ad Mariam'[1] is an entirely remarkable poem in the style of Swinburne, which may indeed have eclipsed its model. It is a poem of five octets written in rather breathless tetrameters; the first two stanzas will illustrate its competence sufficiently for our purpose:

When a sister, born for each strong month-brother,
    Spring's one daughter, the sweet child May,
Lies in the breast of the young year-mother
    With light on her face like the waves at play,
Man from the lips of him speaketh and saith,
At the touch of her wandering wondering breath
Warm on his brow: lo! where is another
    Fairer than this one to brighten our day?

[1] Written in 1884; posthumously published in *Blandyke Papers* in 1890, and four years later in the *Stonyhurst Magazine*.

We have suffered the sons of Winter in sorrow
   And been in their ruinous reigns oppressed,
And fain in the springtime surcease would borrow
   From all the pain of the past's unrest;
And May has come, hair-bound in flowers,
With eyes that smile thro' the tears of the hours,
With joy for to-day and hope for to-morrow
   And the promise of Summer within her breast!

'Winter in the Gulf Stream', written in 1871, is
interesting because it stands like a lonely flower amid
the fallow land of his seven years poetical silence. It
reminds us somewhat of the magic of Mr. De la Mare,
and yet simultaneously it faintly foreshadows that
castigation and white-hot austerity which characterizes
his later work; a fact which will be easily seen from
these concluding lines of the poem:

early compared with late

   A simple passage of weak notes
   Is all the winter bird dare try.
   The moon, half-orbed, ere sunset floats
      So glassy white above the sky,
   So like a berg of hyaline
   And pencilled blue so daintily,
      I never saw her so divine.
   But through black branches, rarely drest
   In streaming scarfs that smoothly shine.
      Shot o'er with lights the emblazon'd west
   Where yonder crimson fireball sets
   Trails forth a purpled-silken vest.
   · Long beds I see of violets
   In beryl lakes which they reef o'er.
   A Pactolean river frets

Against the tawny-golden shore.,
All ways the molten colours run
Till sinking ever more and more
Into an azure mist the sun
Drops down engulfed: his journey done.

At the end of 1875 came the 'Wreck of the Deutsch-land',[1] and with it the clear manifestation of his future greatness. It is the longest and one of the greatest of the poems and contains in miniature all the virtues (and faults) of his more mature work. In a letter to R. W. Dixon, 1878, he tells of its birth, which, as it is the real genesis of his greater poetry, is of no small interest:

What I had written I burnt before I became a Jesuit [2] and resolved to write no more, as not belonging to my profession, unless it were by the wish of my superiors; so for seven years I wrote nothing but two or three little presentation pieces which occasion called for. But when in the winter of '75 the *Deutschland* was wrecked in the mouth of the Thames and five Franciscan nuns, exiles from Germany by the Falck Laws, aboard of her were drowned I was affected by the account and happening to say so to my rector he said he wished some one would write a poem on the subject. On this hint I set to work and, though my hand was out at first, produced one. I had long had haunting my ear the echo of a new rhythm which now I

a new rhythm

---

[1] This poem and subsequent ones in this and the succeeding chapter, unless otherwise stated are taken from *Poems of Gerard Manley Hopkins*, edited by Robert Bridges.   [2] In 1868.

realized on paper. . . . I do not say the idea is altogether new . . . but no one has professedly used it and made it the principle throughout, that I know of.[1]

The principles of the 'new rhythm', enucleated five years afterwards, were printed by the Laureate as a preface to the poems. They are a curious admixture of established principles and valuable neologisms. Movement arising from iambics Hopkins terms Rising Rhythm; from trochaics, Falling Rhythm; from amphibrachs, Rocking Rhythm. For purposes of scansion he would have us consider the stress always first in a foot, as in a musical bar, so that there will be two fundamental uniform rhythms only, the Trochaic and the Dactyllic.[2] When trochees and dactyls occur in the same line, a composite rhythm arises called, after the Greeks, a logaoedic Rhythm. His poetry is filled with such examples, as:

> Down in dim woods the diamond delves! the elves'-
> eyes![3]

or

> Those lovely lads once, wet-fresh windfalls of war's
> storm.[4]

---

[1] A subsequent sentence illustrates a classical example of editorial timidity: 'However I had to mark the stresses . . . and a great many more oddnesses could not but dismay an editor's eye, so that when I offered it to our magazine *The Month* . . . they dared not print it.'

[2] Lest this offend orthodox prosodists who hold (rightly) that English rhythm is fundamentally iambic, it should be remembered that Hopkins suggests this only as a *device* for scansion. Moreover the remaining principles require this to be in harmony with accepted canons.

[3] 'The Starlight Night.'

[4] 'To What Serves Mortal Beauty?'

or

> Márgarét áre you gríeving
> Over Goldengrove unleaving?
> Leáves, líke the things of man, you
> With your fresh thoughts care for, can you?
> Áh! ás the heárt gróws older,[1] &c.

But because unswerving adherence to uniform rhythm would only result in a metronomic sameness, Hopkins introduces licences and irregularities to give variety and pleasure. These are a substitution of arsis for thesis and *e contra*—called Reversed Feet—which, when united, induce a superimposed rhythm. Thus there are two existing rhythms in the ear and mind and the ensemble he calls Counterpoint Rhythm, on the analogy of counterpoint in music. Thus the reversed foot in:

> God lover of souls, *swaying* considerate scales [2]

or the contrapuntal effects of:

> *Wind-beat white-beam! airy abeles* set on a flare![3]

or

> *By that window* what task what fingers ply [4]

or

> *Innocent mind and May-day* in girl and boy,[5] &c.

In addition to Running (or Common) Rhythm and Counterpoint Rhythm, Hopkins invents a still more subtle, flexible and masterly movement which he calls 'Sprung' Rhythm. It occurs when Running Rhythm

[1] 'Spring and Fall.'   [2] 'In the Valley of the Elwy.'
[3] 'The Starlight Night.'   [4] 'The Candle Indoors.'   [5] 'Spring.'

is counterpointed throughout and as only one of the counter-rhythms is heard, the other is really destroyed. Sprung Rhythm contains regularly from one to four syllables in each foot, and for particular effects any number of weak syllables. The stress falls on the first syllable and gives rise to four variations of the same fundamental movement: monosyllabic feet, Trochaic, Dactyllic, and First Paeonic ($- \cup \cup \cup$). A typical example of monosyllabic feet can be found in 'Hurrahing in Harvest':

> The heart rears wings bold and bolder

which may be scanned

$$\cup - \mid - \mid - \mid - \cup \mid - \cup$$

Thus Sprung Rhythm differs from Running Rhythm in being essentially logaoedic, and in being one generic movement instead of three. This difference in movement may be seen by comparing the following quatrain in Running Rhythm:

> The world is charged with the grandeur of God.
> It will flame out like shining from shook foil;
> It gathers to a greatness like the ooze of oil
> Crushed. Why do men then now not reck his rod? [1]

with the following quatrain in Sprung Rhythm:

> And azuring-over greybell makes
> Woodbanks and brakes wash wet like lakes
> And magic cuckoocall
> Caps, clears, and clinches all— [2]

Sprung Rhythm will not admit of contrapuntal

---

[1] 'God's Grandeur.'   [2] 'The May Magnificat.'

variations (as is evident from its nature) though it will admit of pauses, as in the line:

> ... to keep
> Back beauty, keep it, beauty, beauty, *beauty* ... from
> vanishing away?[1]

Sprung Rhythm will also admit of *hangers* or *out-riders*, which are unaccented syllables added to a foot to give hesitancy or swiftness, or airiness, or heaviness, &c., though these syllables do not count in the nominal scanning. An admirable example may be found in the second line of:

> I caught this morning morning's minion, king-
> dom of daylight's dauphin, *dapple-dawn-drawn-*
> *Falcon, in his* riding[2]

or in the line

> Cuckoo-echoing, bell-swarmèd, lark-charmèd, rock-
> racked, river-rounded.[3]

This schematic simplification which I have been endeavouring to elaborate may be illustrated by the following diagram:

[1] 'The Leaden Echo.' [2] 'The Windhover.'
[3] 'Duns Scotus's Oxford.' [4] Stress = thesis; slack = arsis.

So profound, yet simple, an analysis of English Prosody is an important and indeed a magnificent contribution to the more scholarly phase of English Literature. For those of (seemingly) more straitened vision or superficial requirements who would relegate it to an esoteric few as impracticable, it were well to recall Hopkins's own note on Sprung Rhythm which, as he tells us,

> is the most natural of things. For (1) it is the rhythm of common speech and of written prose, when rhythm is perceived in them. (2) It is the rhythm of all but the most monotonously regular music so that in the words of choruses and refrains and in songs written closely to music it arises. (3) It is found in nursery rhymes, weather saws. . . . (4) It arises in common verse when reversed or counter-pointed for the same reason.

Historically Sprung Rhythm has noble ancestry. It occurs as Hopkins rightly suggests, as early as *Piers Ploughman* and extends itself through the Elizabethans as far as Greene who is 'the last writer who can be said to have recognized it'. However it seems to us impossible to limit it even to these boundaries, for if Greene wrote:

> Sitting by a river's side,
> Where a silent stream did glide,
> More I did of many things
> That the mind in quiet brings.
> I 'gan think how some men deem
> Gold their god; and some esteem

Honour is the chief content
That to man in life is lent;
    And some others do contend
    Quiet none like to a friend[1].

Beaumont and Fletcher could write after his death:

All ye woods and trees and bow'rs,
All ye virtues and ye pow'rs
That inhabit in the lakes,
In the pleasant springs or brakes,
        Move your feet
        To our sound,
        Whilst we greet
        All this ground,
With his honour and his name
That defends our flocks from blame.[2]

And Donne:

Till then, Love, let my body range, and let
Me travel, sojourn, snatch, plot, have, forget,
Resume my last year's relict . . . .[3]

And Herbert:

Throw away Thy rod,
Throw away Thy wrath;
    O my God,
Take the gentle path!
For my heart's desire
Unto Thine is bent:
    I aspire
To a full consent.

---

[1] 'Philomela's Ode.'   [2] 'Song to Pan.'   [3] 'Love's Usury.'

And Herrick:

> Welcome maids of honour,
> You do bring
> In the spring,
> And wait upon her.

And Blake:

> Thou fair-haired Angel of the Evening,
> Now whilst the sun rests on the mountains, light
> Thy bright torch of love—thy radiant crown
> Put on, and smile upon our evening bed!
> Smile on our loves: and while thou drawest the
> Blue curtains of the sky, scatter thy silver dew
> On every flower that shuts its sweet eyes
> In timely sleep.[1]

Milton, too, is 'the great Master' of contrapu tal variations, a fact which Hopkins was the first to point out. Thus we find in 'Samson Agonistes' such lines as the fourth in the following:

> Desire of wine and all delicious drinks,
> Which many a famous warrior overturns,
> Thou couldst repress; nor did the dancing ruby,
> Sparkling, out-poured, the flavour or the smell
> Or taste, that cheer the heart of gods and men
> Allure thee from the cool crystalline stream.

But to return to the craftsman himself. Hopkins was aware that, unimpeachable as his theory was, his execution was not always of unalloyed perfection, that there were occasional shortcomings, artistic lapses, 'grubs in amber'. Even granting the premises that his

---

[1] 'To The Evening Star.'

H

readers should 'take breath and read it with the ears, as I always wish to be read', it would be difficult to justify artistically such rhymes as:

> England . . . mingle and; behaviour . . . gave you a; ride and jar, did . . . disregarded; boon he on . . . communion; burn all . . . eternal; I am and . . . d'_a-mond; &c.

or even to accept such rhymes as:

> wrecked her? he . . . electric; busy to . . . unvisited; justices . . . eye he is.

Improving on the common principle of 'enjambed lines', Hopkins tells us that in Sprung Rhythm the lines may be 'rove over'. To take an example, in the following quatrain 'Sire-he-shares' should be read quickly to harmonize with its counterpart, 'Irish':

> A Bugler boy from barrack (it is over the hill
> There)—boy bugler, born, he tells me, of Irish
>   Mother to an English sire (he
> Shares their best gifts surely, fall how things will)[1]

Intriguing as such a principle is, yet even in the hands of a great master it tends of its nature to destroy the rhythmic or at least the rhyming architectural substructure, if it does not indeed degenerate into a quasi-apocope. This latter is often found in light versification, and occasionally in the more serious work of the 'Metaphysicals'. Hopkins uses it in seven places:

> . . . For earth her being has unbound, her dapple is at an end, *as-*
> *tray* or aswarm, all throughter, in throngs; . . .[2]

[1] 'A Bugler's First Communion.'   [2] 'Spelt from Sibyl's Leaves.

or

> To what serves mortal beauty—dangerous; does set
>   *danc-*
>   *ing* blood . . .[1]

or

> . . . plead nor do I: I *wear-*
>   *y* of idle a being . . . .[2]

or

> How then should Gregory, a father, have gleanéd
>   else from *swarm-*
> *ed* Rome? . . .[3]

or

> Cloud-puffball, torn tufts, tossed pillows flaunt
>   forth, then chevy on an *air-*
> *built* thoroughfare;[4]

or

> I caught this morning morning's minion *King-*
>   *dom* of daylight's dauphin . . .[5]

though there seems to be an intellectual as well as a euphonic justification in the following:

> . . . Fury had shrieked 'No *ling-*
> *ering!* Let me be fell: force I must be brief.'[6]

There is another licence which, though common in the ancients and especially in Homer, makes for obscurity in Hopkins's work. It is the employment of 'tmesis' for rhythmical emphasis. Thus in the 'Deutschland' for 'brimful in a flash', he writes: 'brim, in a flash,

[1] 'Mortal Beauty.'   [2] No. 44.
[3] 'Mortal Beauty.'   [4] 'Nature is a Heraclitean Fire.'
[5] 'The Windhover.'   [6] No. 41.

full!'; or again in 'Harry Ploughman' for 'wind-laced lilylocks' he writes: 'See his wind-lilylocks-laced!'; or again in the 'Sibyl' he writes: 'sheathe- and shelterless'.

But his most characteristic and original peculiarity, as Dr. Bridges has pointed out, is in the omission of the relative:

> . . . . Here! creep,
> Wretch, under a comfort [that] serves in a whirl-
> wind.[1]
> After-comers cannot guess the beauty [that has]
> been.[2]
> O Hero [that] savest.[3]
> Squander the hell-rook ranks [that] sally to molest
> him.[4]

There is also the verbal obscurity of an occasional syncopation as 'throughter' for 'through the other', and an occasional homophonetic doubt as in 'have fair fallen' where 'have' is an imperative and not an auxiliary. Then again we find doubtful analyses in such lines as: 'your round me roaming end' [end your roaming round me], or 'to own my heart' [to my own heart], or 'under be my boughs' [be under my boughs], or 'as skies betweenpie mountains' which Dr. Bridges ingeniously explains: 'as the sky seen between dark mountains is brightly dappled'.

Hopkins will also maroon prepositions, a use of which I can find no exact counterpart in any other poet:

> The vault and scope and schooling
> And mastery in the mind,

---

[1] No. 41.   [2] 'Binsey Poplars.'
[3] 'Eurydice.'   [4] 'The Bugler's First Communion.'

In silk-ash kept from cooling,
And ripest under rind—
What life half lifts the latch of,
What hell stalks towards the snatch of,
Your offering, with dispatch, of ! [1]

Hopkins's craftsmanship seized upon the sonnet
as its own peculiar province, radiating into the
extraordinary excursions of his wonted originality.
Out of forty-five complete poems written after the
'Deutschland', thirty-four are sonnets. Of these, two
are Curtal, three Caudated, eight with six beats to
the line, and the whole either 'counterpointed' or
'sprung'. Probably the simplest construction in any of
the sonnets is in 'The Lantern out of Doors'; here the
octet is regular throughout, but the sestet has its first
line 'counterpointed', its fifth line 'sprung', and the
intermediate lines hexasyllabic. To quote a more
interesting, though equally simple, example, we find
in 'Spring' that only one line is a strict iambic penta-
meter; but the changes will be seen to be almost
necessary adjuncts to both thought and rhythm.

Nothing is so beautiful as spring   *catalectic*
    When weeds, in wheels, shoot long   *substitution*
        and lovely and lush;
    Thrush's eggs look little low heavens,   *catalectic*
        and thrush
Through the echoing timber does so   *substitution*
        rinse and wring
The ear, it strikes like lightnings to hear   *substitution*
        him sing;

        [1] 'Morning, Midday and Evening Sacrifice.'

The glassy peartree leaves and blooms,
   they brush
The descending blue; that blue is all in   *substitution*
   a rush
With richness; the racing lambs too have   *substitution*
   fair their fling.
What is all this juice and all this joy?   *catalectic*
   A strain of the earth's sweet being in   *substitution &*
   the beginning   *hypermetric*
In Eden garden.—Have, get, before it   *substitution*
   cloy,
   Before it cloud, Christ, lord, and sour   *hypermetric*
   with sinning,
Innocent mind and Mayday in girl and boy   *counterpointed*
   Most, O maid's child, thy choice and   *counterpointed*
   worthy the winning.

Passing from the simplest to the most difficult, we
find his greatest metrical achievement in 'The Windhover'. It exhausts all the richness of his great prosodic
system, and in it he seems to have reached the final
boundaries of rhythmic possibility—any further would
result in a sheer cleavage of rhythm and meaning. It
also furnishes another perfect illustration of the power
of craftsmanship to whip a rigid and inflexible form
into action, and to endow it with immanent suppleness.
To attain this difficult end he almost confounds us with
his sprung rhythm, falling paeons, outrides, rocking
rhythm, monosyllabic feet, catalectic inflexions:

I caught this morning morning's minion, king-
   dom of daylight's dauphin, dapple-dawn-drawn
   Falcon, in his riding

Of the rolling level underneath him steady air, and
    striding
High there, how he rung upon the rein of a wimpling
    wing
In his ecstacy! then off, off forth in swing,
    As a skate's heel sweeps smooth on a bow-bend: the
    hurl and gliding
Rebuffed the big wind. My heart in hiding
Stirred for a bird,—the achieve of, the mastery of the
    thing!

Brute beauty and valour and act, oh, air, pride, plume,
    here
    Buckle! AND the fire that breaks from thee then, a
    billion
Times told lovelier, more dangerous, O my chevalier!
    No wonder of it: shéer plod makes plough down
    sillion
Shine, and blue-bleak embers, ah my dear,
    Fall, gall themselves, and gash gold-vermilion.

As we are now concerned with the architectural
analysis only, it may be in place to show the rhythmical
skeleton of the poem and to tabulate some of the principles used therein:

Scansion	Principle
∪ – | ∪ – | ∪ – | ∪ – | ∪ – |	Iambic pentameter, rove over
– ∪ ∪ ∪ | – ∪ | – ∪ ∪ ∪ | – ∪ ∪ ∪ | – ∪ |	First Paeonic
– ∪ ∪ ∪ | – ∪ ∪ ∪ | – ∪ ∪ ∪ | – ∪ | – ∪ |	First Paeonic, crescendo
– ∪ ∪ ∪ | – ∪ ∪ ∪ | – ∪ ∪ | – ∪ | – ⌒ |	First Paeonic, diminuendo, rove over
∪ | ∪ – ∪ | – | ∪ – | ∪ – | ∪ – |	Rocking Rhythm, sprung monosyllabic

∪∪−∪∪ | − | ∪∪−∪∪ | −∪ | −∪ | Rocking Rhythm, sprung monosyllabic

∪− | ∪− | −∧ | ∪− | ∪− | ∪ | Catalectic, Hypermetric

−∪∪ | −∪∪ | −∪∪ | −∪∪∪∪ | − | Hangers, sprung mono- syllabic

∪−∪∪ | −∪∪ | −∪ | −−∪ | −∪ | Second Paeonic

−∪ | −∪∪∪ | −∪∪ | −∪ | −∪ | First Paeonic

−∪ | −∪∪∪ | −∪∪ | −∪∪∪ | − | First Paeonic

∪ | −∪∪∪ | − | −∪ | −∪ | −∪ | First Paeonic, sprung monosyllabic

−∪ | −∪ | −∪ | −∪ | − | Sprung monosyllabic

− | −∪∪∪ | − | −∪ | −∪ | Sprung monosyllabic and First Paeonic

Hopkins's caudated sonnets find their prototype in Milton. Comparing 'Tom's Garland' with Milton's sonnet 'On the New Forcers of Conscience', we find an identical rhyme-scheme; and two codas form two tercets, the beginning line of each being an iambic trimeter and the two succeeding lines penta-meters, with the rhyming scheme *abb, bcc*. However, in 'Harry Ploughman' and 'That Nature is a Hera-clitean Fire' Hopkins enters into his own province. The former consists of nineteen lines, with three shortened added lines intermittently placed in the octet, and a shortened line added to each tercet in the sestet. The third sonnet consists of twenty-four six-foot lines, the last ten of which are caudated in the following manner:

. . . nor mark
Is any of him at all so stark
But vastness blurs and time beats level. Enough! the Resurrection,
A heart's clarion! Away grief's gasping, joyless days, dejection.

Across my foundering deck shone

A beacon, an eternal beam. Flesh fade, and mortal
    trash
Fall to the residuary worm; world's wildfire, leave but
    ash:

In a flash, at a trumpet crash,

I am all at once what Christ is, since he was what I am,
    and
This Jack, joke, poor potsherd, patch, matchwood,
    immortal diamond,

Is immortal diamond.

So remarkable a use of the three coda-ed ending
may, in part, justify the change in the sonnet-form.
But the two Curtal sonnets, it seems, can be admitted
to the title only by analogy. 'Pied Beauty', in the
major part, consists of six lines, in the minor part of
four lines to which is added a 'half-line tailpiece' or
dimeter, and having a rhyme-scheme of *abc, abc, dbcd,
c*. The metre is sprung, the feet Falling Paeonic, with
four beats to the line, as:

$$-\cup\cup\cup\,|\,-\cup\,|\,-\cup\,|\,-$$

Glory be to God for dappled things—

$$\cup\,|\,-\cup\cup\cup\,|\,-\cup\cup\cup\,|\,-\cup\,|\,-$$

For skies of couple-colour as a brinded cow.

'Peace' has a similar construction, with the rhyme-
scheme *abc, abc, dcbd, c*, the lines Alexandrine, and
the 'half-line tailpiece' a trimeter. Its beginning lines
run:

When will you ever, Peace, wild wooddove, shy wings
    shut,
Your round me roaming end, and under be my boughs?

and its concluding lines:

O surely, reaving Peace, my Lord should leave in lieu
Some good! And so he does leave Patience exquisite,
That plumes to Peace thereafter. And when Peace
    here does house
He comes with work to do, he does not come to coo,
    He comes to brood and sit.

To say anything further about the remaining poems seems unnecessary in view of the principles and their application already considered. We have attempted to draw aside the veil of Gerard Hopkins's obscurity and to look upon the extraordinary structure of his theory of his prosody. It is only with a fuller realization of this that the grammatical uncertainties and metrical oddities will divide and rinse clear. And what before seemed 'masses of impracticable quartz' may now become a jewel-case marvellously wrought and lovely to behold, a monstrance, as it were, for a Living Flame. It is this preliminary ascesis which is the price of a thorough appreciation of poetry of such specialized significance; and just as the fear of the initial effort involved has led some aspirants to easier and less-worthy poets, so imperfect discipline in it has led other readers to attain only a partial and therefore less-worthy acceptance. It is this which has resulted in that strange anomaly existent in all the fine arts, of a genius who commands respect and enthusiasm from those who possess an 'ascetic' aestheticism, but who receives neglect or even abuse from those who will not, or cannot, 'plough the rock until it bear!' Gerard Hopkins will always call forth great praise and great blame.

VII

THE ARTIST

'The fine delight that fathers thought.'

G. M. H.

IF one follow Gerard Hopkins through the several
phases of his poetic evolution it seems difficult to
reconcile the writer of 'The Habit of Perfection' with
that of 'The Wreck of the Deutschland'. The
enormity and suddenness of the change have but one
parallel example—that of 'The Angel in the House'
and 'The Unknown Eros'—but in Patmore the new
style was not entirely chastened, nor did it as often
reach final perfection in him, as it did in Hopkins.
Succeeding phases in the latter's development are like
those of any other great mind in art, the more facile play
of a creative and growing faculty, the gradual passing
from obscurantism to a more profound simplicity.

The obscurity, which primarily besets his artistry,
springs from two causes; the one from the difficulty in
attaining the almost unattainable ideal of his craftsmanship, the other, as in Donne, from the nature of his
thought. This second difficulty was again different
from that of his contemporaries, say, from Browning's
tortuous and often misty sequence; it sprang rather
from the depth of his thought, so that (to use a striking
phrase of Mr. Middleton Murry) his was 'not so much
a triumph of language as a victory over language'.[1]
His obscurity also differs from that of many of the

[1] *The Problem of Style*, p. 94.

moderns. A certain preternatural elusiveness in him is
far from what Mr. Richards has called a 'music of
ideas'[1] in the poetry of Mr. T. S. Eliot. Hopkins wrote
the 'Deutschland' from an intuition of will and intellect, but Mr. Eliot wrote the 'Waste Land' from an
intuition of emotions and impressions which eschew
the logic of ideas. Hopkins will also differ from other
poets of to-day who have attempted a sensuous intuition only. But [however obscure the intellectual
intuition of his appeal, yet it does not leave his work
mere skeletal thought loosely covered with laboured
prettinesses and rhythmical arabesques, but rather an
intimate fusion wrung from imperishable blows, an
interior and subtle rhythm which, in the final analysis,
make his lines inevitably ring true.

'The Wreck of the Deutschland' stands, as Dr.
Bridges has pointed out, 'chronologically as well as
logically in front of his book, like a great dragon
folded in the gate to forbid all entrance.' It is a poem
which shares the mysteriousness of Thompson's
'Mistress of Vision', the mysticism of 'The Hound of
Heaven', and that indefinable, impalpable, dramatic
starkness of the ' Prometheus' of Aeschylus.]It is also
of extreme importance in discerning the influences to
which his work was subjected. Writing, as he did, after
a period of poetic inaction and girt with the new
rhythm and metre, his attention was more concerned
with technical liberation and emotional expression than
with conscious originality. The spirit of the whole
poem (as, indeed, of most of his poetry) is more
closely allied to the seventeenth century than the nine-

[1] *Principles of Literary Criticism*, p. 293.

teenth, though there are momentary flashes that faintly
remind us of such contemporaries as Tennyson:

Thy unchancelling poising palms were weighing the
    worth,
        Thou martyr-master: in thy sight
Storm flakes were scroll-leaved flowers, lily showers—
    sweet heaven was astrew in them.

or Browning:

       ... Is out with it! Oh,
        We lash with the best or worst
       Word last!
       But how shall I ... make me room there:
        Reach me a ... Fancy, come faster—
      Strike you the sight of it? look at it loom there,
        Thing that she ... there then! the Master,
    Ipse, the only one, Christ, King, Head:

or Morris:

       Away in the loveable west,
       On a pastoral forehead of Wales.

or Swinburne:

Thou knowest the walls, altar and hour and night:
The swoon of a heart that the sweep and the hurl of
    thee trod
Hard down with a horror of height.

    I whirled out wings that spell
And fled with a fling of the heart to the heart of the Host
My heart, but you were dovewinged I can tell,

    .   .   .   .   .   .

To flash from the flame to the flame then, tower from
    the grace to the grace.

or earlier writers as Shelley:

> I kiss my hand
> To the stars, lovely-asunder
> Starlight, wafting him out of it; . . .

or Donne:

> I am soft sift
> In an hour-glass—at the wall
> Fast, but mined with a motion. . . .

There is something of the spirit of Milton in these lines:

> . . . the jay-blue heavens appearing
> Of pied and peeled May!

Such quotations are, of course, not mere imitations, but they do suggest influences however remote or evanescent. The remarkable thing is that so many diverse (and there are more!) styles could be fused into an unmistakable whole. His methods, though more skilled, in this poem remind us somewhat of Browning's—an internal versatility, the union of several distinct styles, the juxtaposition of vigour and euphony.

The emotional content in 'The Deutschland' is very great. Its first lines burst into a magnificent apostrophe to the Creatorship, Providence, and Mastery of God, so great that the Shelley of 'The Wild West Wind' might have written their impassioned fervour. Thence it passes to the action of the Creator upon men, thence to the problem of suffering which 'rides time like riding a river', and through the medium of Scotist theology sees it consequent on the Incarnation (verse 7). The last two stanzas of Part One are a recapitulation and a key to the whole poem; the following quotation will illustrate this, and at the same time characterize the new-born rhythm with its sprung leadings in four lines and sprung rhythm in one (the fifth):

> Be adored among men,
> God, three-numberéd form;
> Wring thy rebel, dogged in den,
> Man's malice, with wrecking and storm.
> Beyond saying sweet, past telling of tongue,
> Thou art lightning and love, I found it, a winter and warm;
> Father and fondler of heart thou hast wrung:
> Hast thy dark descending and most art merciful then.

The Second Part is exactly two and a half times the length of the first and is concerned with the imagined scene on the doomed ship. Its leaping lines bring us back to William Falconer who was wrecked in the Aegean and who subsequently published 'The Shipwreck' in 1762. His description is more detailed and expert than Hopkins's, but its grandiloquence and lack of artistry would make any comparison *perverse*. There is something final and satisfying in the wild poignancy of such lines as:

> One stirred from the rigging to save
> The wild woman-kind below,
> With a rope's end round the man, handy and brave—
> He was pitched to his death at a blow,
> For all his dreadnought breast and braids of thew:
> They could tell him for hours, dandled the to and fro

Through the cobbled foam-fleece, what could he do
With the burl of the fountains of air, buck and the
    flood of the wave?
They fought with God's cold—
And they could not and fell to the deck
(Crushed them) or water (and drowned them)
    or rolled
With the sea-romp over the wreck.
Night roared, with the heart-break hearing a heart-
    broke rabble,
The woman's wailing, the crying of child without
    check—
Till a lioness arose breasting the babble,
A prophetess towered in the tumult, a virginal tongue
    told.

Apart from the many individual marvellous lines
which spangle the whole poem, one cannot refrain
from a last quotation which may take its place among
any lines in Tennyson for vowel-music and slow
grandeur, and which carry further the thought in
Shelley's 'Adonais' ('The One remains, the many
change and pass'):

I admire thee, master of the tides,
    Of the Yore-flood, of the year's fall;
The recurb and the recovery of the gulf's sides,
    The girth of it and the wharf of it and the wall;
Staunching, quenching ocean of a motionable mind;
Ground of being, and granite of it: past all
    Grasp God, throned behind
Death with a sovereignty that heeds but hides, bodes
    but abides.

'The Deutschland' is the companion poem to another elegy, written also for those drowned at sea, 'The Loss of the Eurydice'. But reading the second poem is like turning from Shelley to Wordsworth. 'The Deutschland' with its remarkable verse-construction, its plangent emotion, its directness, is like the majestic sweep of an ocean-wave; 'The Eurydice' is subdued, recollected in tranquillity, and artistically the least perfect of all his work. Its rhymes are often forced, its metric construction hampers its freedom, the craftsman is everywhere in evidence, though his genius is generally triumphant. Hopkins himself recognized the presence of a certain 'raw nakedness' in the poem, but the defect, he claimed, was a visual one and could be removed by an auditory reading. He wrote: 'Indeed when, on somebody returning me the *Eurydice*, I opened and read some lines, as one commonly reads whether prose or verse, with the eyes, so to say, only, it struck me aghast with a kind of raw nakedness and unmitigated violence I was unprepared for; but take breath and read it with the ears, as I always wish to be read, and my verse becomes all right.' Approaching the poem in this way, the difficulties will vanish, and in their place, the internal onomatopoeic delicacy and sheer magic of such lines as:

> And flockbells off the aerial
> Downs' forefalls beat to the burial;

or what Dixon called 'Grecian' in:

> And you were a liar, O blue March day.
> Bright sun lanced fire in the heavenly bay;

I

or the reminiscence of Virgil's Palinurus, *summa sub-limis ab unda*,[1] in the lines:

> Now he shoots short up to the round air;
> Now he gasps, now he gazes everywhere.

'The Loss of the Eurydice' and 'The Loss of the Royal George' have a similar origin, and it is interesting to compare the swift vigour of Hopkins with the comparative tameness of Cowper. Where the latter writes:

> Eight hundred of the brave,
>   Whose courage well was tried,
> Had made the vessel heel,
>   And laid her on her side.
> A land breeze shook the shrouds,
>   And she was overset;
> Down went the Royal George,
>   With all her crew complete.

Hopkins writes:

> Too proud, too proud, what a press she bore!
> Royal, and all her royals wore.
>   Sharp with her, shorten sail!
> Too late; lost; gone with the gale.
>
> This was that fell capsize,
> As half she had righted and hoped to rise
>   Death teeming in by her portholes
> Raced down decks, round messes of mortals.
>
> Then a lurch forward, frigate and men;
> 'All hands for themselves' the cry ran then;
>   But she who had housed them thither
> Was around them, bound them or wound them with her.

[1] *Aeneid* vi. 357.

Turning to a wider survey of Hopkins's works we note a fundamental simplicity in his art from which emanate the various avenues of varied forms. In the simple and straightforward lyrics the guileless artistry of the early poems makes a marked contrast with the highly-wrought artistry of his later work. There is a world of difference between the artistic simplicity of the two following quatrains:

> Elected Silence, sing to me
> And beat upon my whorléd ear,
> Pipe me to pastures still and be
> The music that I care to hear.

> Thee, God, I come from, to thee go,
> All day long I like fountain flow
> From thy hand out, swayed about
> Mote-like in thy mighty glow.

The first is merely beautiful, the second (written twenty years later) is strong, poised, final. This is similar also to the change from the formal beauty of the 'Rosa Mystica'[1] or 'May Magnificat' to that of 'The Blessed Virgin Compared to the Air We Breathe'. The last poem demands leisure and meditation. It is a miracle of artistic simplicity, and the mystic import in the third stanza makes it an achievement in Marian poetry almost unrivalled and never surpassed except perhaps by the sublime prose-poems in the writings of St. Bernard. Even Francis Thompson's 'Mistress of Vision' with its marvellous mysteriousness falls short of this with

---

[1] This poem like the 'May Magnificat' and the 'Ad Mariam' were hung before the Lady Statue at Stonyhurst College in May, along with other local contributions. The occasion called for natural simplicity rather than art.

its theological content and its terrifying, mystical directness. Hopkins's poem is more comparable to the great Marian poem of Fray Luis de Leon of the sixteenth century though the latter is more extensive than intensive in form.

The sonnets, too, share in this evolutionary simplification. There is great art in:

And for all this, nature is never spent;
   There lives the dearest freshness deep down things;
And though the last lights off the black West went
   Oh, morning, at the brown brink eastward,
      springs—
Because the Holy Ghost over the bent
   World broods with warm breast and with ah! bright
      wings.[1]

But there is far greater art in the following sestet written about ten years later:

O the mind, mind has mountains; cliffs of fall
Frightful, sheer, no-man-fathomed. Hold them cheap
May who ne'er hung there. Nor does long our small
Durance deal with that steep or deep. Here! creep,
Wretch, under a comfort serves in a whirlwind: all
Life death does end and each day dies with sleep.[2]

In his greater sonnets this simplification is always at work. 'The Windhover' is more direct than most critics have allowed, for it seems that they have sometimes woven into it complexities which were foreign to the author's intention. It is a poem which hangs like a pendant from one word, the verb 'buckle'. The

[1] 'God's Grandeur'.   [2] No. 41.

octet is a statement of fact, a striking picture of the achievement and mastery of a Windhover in a 'big wind'. There are added superficial embellishments as, for instance, the three liquids sentinelled by the two strong gutturals in the first line; the unfolding of the dentals and long vowels in the second line; the incredible onomatopoeia in the central lines. The sestet is a reflection on the buckling of 'brute beauty and valour and act, oh, air, pride, plume' in the bird, which breaks into a fiery beauty 'a billion times told lovelier' than before. Then he adds the reason, that the potential beauty hiding beneath all things breaks forth 'a billion times told lovelier' when it is stirred into action, even as:

> . . . blue-bleak embers, ah my dear,
> Fall, gall themselves, and gash gold-vermilion.

He said in 1879 that it was 'the best thing I ever wrote', and therefore he dedicated it to 'Christ our Lord'. It is the only titled sonnet with a dedication. Ten years after the writing of the 'Windhover', he composed his 'That Nature is a Heraclitean Fire and of the comfort of the Resurrection', which, to me, seems to stand first among his triumphs and which also has the customary simplification. Its extraordinary ending has at last rivalled the serene exaltation of the close of Browning's 'Prospice'. Closely related to this sonnet is 'Spelt from Sibyl's Leaves' which is fraught with calculated rhythms and striking lines, but which is restrained and subdued; the two sonnets are like two soaring rockets, one trailing a blaze of light only, the other breaking into a cascade of stars.

Of the two further species of sonnets little need be said. 'Tom's Garland' and 'Harry Ploughman' are the two exceptions to the process of simplification, and without a commentary withstand every form of intellectual strategy on the part of the reader. Hopkins apparently did not realize the dire extent of his obscurity; he wrote playfully on 10 February 1888, to Robert Bridges: 'I laughed outright and often, but very sardonically, to think you and the Canon could not construe my last sonnet; that he had to write to you for a crib. It is plain I must go no further on this road; if you and he cannot understand me who will?' The last species of sonnets, published as the posthumous sonnets, have caused much comment, not on account of their technique (for in this they are outstanding and transparent) but for the travail of soul expressed in them. This, as not belonging to the present chapter, will be discussed later, and so we will only point out the climactic crisis in the last line of 'Carrion Comfort', which seems to have no equal in English lyricism.

Not, I'll not, carrion comfort, Despair, not feast on thee;
Not untwist—slack they may be—these last strands
    of man
In me or, most weary, cry *I can no more.* I can;
Can something, hope, wish day come, not choose not
    to be.
But ah, but O thou terrible, why wouldst thou rude
    on me
Thy wring-world right foot rock? lay a lion limb
    against me? scan

With darksome devouring eyes my bruisèd bones?
    and fan
O in turns of tempest, me heaped there; me frantic to
    avoid thee and flee?
Why? That my chaff might fly; my grain lie, sheer
    and clear.
Nay in all that toil, that coil, since (seems) I kissed
    the rod,
Hand rather, my heart lo! lapped strength, stole joy,
    would laugh, chéer.
Cheer whom though? the hero whose heaven-
    handling flung me, fóot tród
Me? or me that fought him? O which one? is it each
    one? That night, that year
Of now done darkness I wretch lay wrestling with (my
    God!) my God.

It is especially in his pastoral poetry that Hopkins
resembles his seventeenth-century predecessors. He
has that flash and quick succession of ideas which mark
the so-called 'Metaphysical' poets, but not their almost
inevitable conceits. Only once does Hopkins tend to
become 'pretious', where, after a line extraordinary in
its marriage of sound and sense, he uses an image
which is discordant in the peculiar field of thought
already engendered:

And the azurous hung hills are his world-wielding
    shoulder
Majestic—as a stallion stalwart, *very violet, sweet*![1]

It is no small tribute to a poet whose originality
must have been hedged round with conceits, to have

    [1] 'Hurrahing in Harvest'.

maintained so daring a course with impunity. The beginning lines of the poem just quoted are flooded with the spirit which inspired Marvell, and the second half of 'Binsey Poplars' might creep almost unobserved into some of Marvell's lines or Vaughan's. However, in his more ecstatic moments in this phase of his poetry, Hopkins's vaulting thought and striking imagery approximate more to the spirit of Crashaw, to the Crashaw more of 'The Shepherd's Hymn' than of 'The Weeper' or 'The Admirable Saint Teresa'. Then too there is an economy worthy of Milton in 'Andromeda', and a real emancipation in this fragment:

> Or like a juicy and jostling shock
> Of bluebells sheaved in May
> Or wind-long fleeces on the flock
> A day off shearing day. [1]

Leaving Milton and going still further back, we note a pleasing union between Hopkins and his Jesuit predecessor, Robert Southwell. They almost sing in unison in:

> Thou who on Sin's wages starvest,
> Behold we have the Joy of Harvest:
> For us was gathered the First-fruits,
> For us was lifted from the roots,
> Sheaved in cruel bands, bruiséd sore,
> Scourged upon the threshing-floor
> Where the upper millstone roofed His Head,
> At morn we found the Heavenly Bread;
> And on a thousand altars laid,
> Christ our Sacrifice is made. [2]

[1] No. 63.   [2] 'Barnfloor and Winepress'.

But Hopkins is more often supremely himself, alone
and inimitable, and his lines ring with the highest of
music and cadence. Sometimes he will pipe a subtle,
purling rhythm as:

> My aspens dear, whose airy cages quelled,
> Quelled or quenched in leaves the leaping sun,
> All felled, felled, are all felled;
> Of a fresh and following folded rank
> Not spared, not one
> That dandled a sandalled
> Shadow that swam or sank
> On meadow and river and wind-wandering weed-
> winding bank.[1]

or deftly startle such magic as:

> In Summer, in a burst of summertime
> Following falls and falls of rain,
> When the air was sweet-and-sour of the flown fine
> flower of
> Those goldnails and their gaylinks that hang along a
> lime; [2]

or with strange harmonies sing:

> Degged with dew, dappled with dew
> Are the groins of the braes that the brook treads
> through,
> Wiry heathpacks, flitches of fern,
> And the beadbonny ash that sits over the burn.[3]

or tinkle dainty music in:

> Tatter-tassel-tangled and dingle-a-dangled
> Dandy-hung dainty head.[4]

[1] 'Binsey Poplars'.   [2] 'Cheery Beggar'.
[3] 'Inversnaid'.   [4] 'The Woodlark'.

or with mounting crescendo sing:

Come then, your ways and airs and looks, locks,
    maiden gear, gallantry and gaiety and grace,
Winning ways, airs innocent, maiden manners, sweet
    looks, loose locks, long locks, lovelocks, gaygear,
    going gallant, girlgrace—
Resign them, sign them, seal them, send them, motion
    them with breath,
And with sighs soaring, soaring sighs deliver
Them; beauty-in-the-ghost, deliver it, early now, long
    before death
Give beauty back, beauty, beauty, beauty, back to
    God, beauty's self and beauty's giver.[1]

Such quotations are representative, though, of course,
not complete. Among other things, they will illustrate
how purely Saxon is Hopkins's vocabulary. His poems
are essentially English, seemingly autochthonous, and
yet they spring from a mind grounded on and
thoroughly disciplined by the culture of ancient
Greece and Rome. Though there is no mention of
any ideal in his notes, yet his work is too flawless to
suppose that it was not always before his mind. This
meticulous care corresponds to the perfection he
demanded from all the other phases of his art, and
complements the character we have been endeavouring
to study in the scope of this chapter.

I have said that Gerard Hopkins's poetry springs
from an original mould of mind, an attractive indi-
viduality. His mental versatility is unceasingly active,
ever working upon the complexity of his craftsman-

[1] 'The Leaden Echo and the Golden Echo.'

ship, the nature of his thought, the ideals of his artistry. The external versatility betrays itself in the construction and varying styles of his work; the internal versatility in the rhythm, the music, the imagination. There is, too, a psychological versatility—his mysteriousness, mysticism, poignancy, tenderness, exaltation, majesty. All these are but modes of a certain dramatic complex in him which makes his work great poetry and which gives to him his vitality and essential humanness. Critical analysis may discover such beauties. But it will not completely exhaust the whole of his artistry, its finality. Perhaps the most perfect symbol of the origin, the function, the destiny of his poetry, is contained in Hopkins's own words:

Glory be to God for dappled things—
    For skies of couple-colour as a brinded cow;
      For rose-moles all in stipple upon trout that swim;
Fresh-firecoal chestnut-falls; finches' wings;
    Landscape plotted and pieced—fold, fallow, and
        plough;
    And all trades, their gear and tackle and trim.

All things counter, original, spare, strange;
    Whatever is fickle, freckled (who knows how?)
      With swift, slow; sweet, sour; adazzle, dim;
He fathers-forth whose beauty is past change:
    Praise him.[1]

---

[1] 'Pied Beauty'.

VIII

THE MAN

God's utterance of Himself in Himself is God the Word, outside Himself is this world. This world then is word, expression, news, of God. Therefore its end, its purpose, its purport, its meaning, is God, and its life or work to name and praise Him.

G. M. H.

THE spirit of Gerard Manley Hopkins rises from the depths of the preceding chapters and stands before us in the light of its creative achievements, its culture, and its friendships. It engenders admiration and respect, but in order to win complete sympathy we propose to complete the picture of his complex personality, to review the remaining facts of his life and character as seen in other writings of his or of his friends.

The story of his boyhood needs no elaboration. The comradeship of a highly-gifted father and the tuition from an artist fittingly prepared him for a life of intensive culture at Oxford. While he was still at Highgate Grammar School we find him in his diaries competently evaluating obscure passages in Servius, Oppian, the Poetics of Aristotle. He was even reading Italian novels! At Oxford his interests were manifold, for, while reading the very heavy syllabus for 'Greats', he was also reading extensively in English and French and German literature; he was studying painting; he was writing on medievalism; he was continually concerned with architecture, and his notes are filled with sketches of an amazing number of churches; he follows the architectural progress of Butterfield (who designed Keble Chapel) through the country; he notes: 'that there is now going on what has no part that I know of in the history of art. . . . The Renaissance appears now to be in the process of being succeeded by a spontaneous Byzantinesque style, retaining still some of the bad features (such as pilasters, rustic work &c.) of the Renaissance. These it will throw aside. Its capitals are already, as in Romanesque art, most beautiful! . . .' He is writing lyrics, ballads, and begins a drama in imitation of the wild grandeur that he saw in *King Lear*. He is ever faithful to record subtle effects in nature, as, for example, 'moonlight hanging on tree-tops like cobwebs.' He reads the poetry written at Oxford in his time and reflects thus:

It is a happy thing that there is no royal road to poetry. The world should know by this time that one cannot reach Parnassus except by flying thither. Yet from time to time more men go up and either perish in its gullies fluttering excelsior flags or else come down again with full folios and blank countenances. Yet the old fallacy keeps its ground. Every age has its false alarms.

He moves in a charming circle of friends, and gives breakfast parties, teas, and dinner parties.

His conversation was clever and incisive [writes an old college friend], and perhaps critical in excess. As to the quality of this criticism I thought much at the time, and have thought much since, that it was the best of the kind to be had in England, in places where production and criticism do not, as is the case at Oxford, keep pace. . . . His acquaintance with poetry was extensive, and his judgements differed upon various poets considerably from what most people entertain.

When I first knew him he called himself a 'Tractarian' on the grounds that he believed Tractarian doctrine true, and if the Church of England rejected it, so much the worse for the Church of England. His leaving it was not to change, but to give expression to his religious faith. . . . Gerard passed first class in Mods., and in the June of 1867, first class in honours in the finals schools. The late Dr. Wilson, his examiner for 'Greats', thought highly of his talents. It was very extraordinary to achieve such success when his mind was preoccupied by the struggles of conversion.

This picture of Hopkins corroborates what the present writer has written elsewhere,[1] that

he was, all his life, a highly original and independent thinker. If he became a fast friend of Newman, it was because he recognized in the older convert more of a kindred spirit than a far-distant leader. . . . If he was a pupil of Pater, as that great critic was then just beginning his own fellowship and as he proceeded M.A. only the year before Hopkins left Oxford, it is probable that the master was still too young and reticent to mould his gifted pupil. . . . Then again Jowett with his seductive liberalism failed to have any permanent influence on his young pupil. Liddon and Pusey, when they discovered that his conver-

[1] *America*, 6 October 1928.

sion was imminent, failed to make Hopkins deviate from the path his subtle reasoning had pointed out. . . .

If it be true that a man's soul with his sentiments and ideals are written on his brow, Gerard Hopkins's meditative countenance suggests the delicate complexion of the spirit within. A contemporary, Rev. W. Lechmere, has given [1] an interesting pen-portrait of Hopkins, which may find a place here:

> One evening I went to the Clarendon Hotel to hear a lecture on the Reformation by a kind of Anglican monk. I was very Protestant in those days and thought to pose him. The occasion indeed is not worth mentioning, but that G. M. Hopkins was also present. It seems, from what Geldart told me, he became interested in me and wished to meet me. I am glad I excited this interest, however undeserved, for otherwise I might never have met one who in the course of a short hour made the impression upon me he did. At this moment, looking back over forty years, I seem to be gazing upon some great portrait of a face, rather than upon a face. What high serenity, what chastened intellectual power, what firm and resigned purpose, and withal what tranquil sadness or perhaps seriousness, suffusing the features rather than casting a shadow upon them! I have no likeness to assist me, but I continue to see the face.

It was at a little luncheon at Geldart's that we

[1] *Oxford and Cambridge Review*, May, 1912.

afterwards met. He said but little, indeed, I only
remember him saying something about one of the
Articles. I saw him but once again, and that only
as we passed in the High. I have but little to go
upon. Some would say I have nothing to go upon,
to which I can only reply that an impression may be
almost instantaneously formed, and that, however
it may be explained, such an impression was formed
in this case. If I may dare to say it, it is in its degree
a 'knowing after the spirit'. Of all I came across at
Oxford, there was not one whose superfineness of
mind and character was more expressed in his entire
bearing.

Such then was Gerard Hopkins when he submitted
himself to the yoke of the Church and the Society
of Jesus. His oblation is extraordinary enough, it
certainly was not unique. That Gerard included with
the holocaust of himself the ashes of his poems, manifests the courageous realization he had of his calling.
Indeed no superior had ever hinted at this immolation
of the poetic instinct, and a few years afterwards his
Rector asked him to write again. But the fact, however
trivial, shows the power that principle played in his
life.

The two years spent at Roehampton were of but
slight external importance. Hopkins fulfilled the office
of Porter with due credit,[1] and preached a panegyric
on St. Stanislaus, the patron of Jesuit novices, which
for its brilliancy and beauty was remembered long
afterwards by those who heard it.

[1] An office concerned with certain details of domestic administration.

In 1870 Hopkins was transferred to St. Mary's Hall, Stonyhurst, to take a three-year course of philosophy, and thence back to Roehampton to teach classics. All the while his diaries continue their faithful recording of impressions. His finely developed sensibilities are never idle. He discerns inscape and instress in all objects—from clouds and flowers and waves to the Castle-Rock at Edinburgh! 'All the world', he says, 'is full of inscape and chance left free to act falls into an order as well as purpose.' And again: 'I thought how surely beauty of inscape was unknown and buried away from simple people and yet how near at hand it was if they had eyes to see it.' And again: 'What you look hard at seems to look hard at you; hence the true and false instress of nature.' Of a flower he says: 'The Horned Violet is a pretty thing, gracefully lashed. Even in withering the flower ran through beautiful inscapes.' He sees the sea 'clothed and purpled all over with wind'.

The inscape of trees particularly appealed to him. Of the leaves in Kew Gardens he says they were 'dimpled in the middle and wonderfully wimpled at the edge'. His elegy on 'Binsey Poplars' tells us how their destruction pained him. He observes 'the felling of trees going on sadly at Roehampton'. And again he says: 'The ashtree growing in the corner of the garden was felled. It was lopped first: I heard the sound and looking out and seeing it maimed there came at that moment a great pang and I wished to die and not to see the inscapes of the world destroyed any more.'

In the spring he goes to the River Hodder and

finds it 'swollen and golden'. Thence to the fells which
were 'all melled and painted with colour and full of
roaming scents and winged silver slips of young
brake'. He listens to the cuckoo singing with 'wonderful, clear, and plump fluty notes', and sees the young
lambs having fair their fling and bounding as to the
tabour's sound: 'They toss and toss; it is as if it were
the earth that flung them, not themselves. It is the
pitch of graceful agility.' He sees pigeons looking like
'little gay jugs by shape when they walk, strutting and
jod-jodding with their heads'. A golden crested wren
flies into his room at night and he 'smoothed and
fingered the little orange and yellow feathers which
are hidden in it. Next morning I found many of these
about the room and enclosed them in a letter to Cyril
on his wedding day'. A naïve gift indeed!

The pages of the diaries are filled with ghost stories;
fairy stories from the lips of those who 'had seen the
fairies'; he reflects often on dreams: 'the dream images
also appear to have little or no projection, to be flat
like pictures, and often one seems to be holding one's
eyes close to them.' He records dialectal importations
from Ireland, Wales, Lancashire, Malta, and even from
the tribes of Lake Uganda. Biela's comet swims into
his ken and he discusses its astrological import with
Father Perry. Some one told him that certain yellow
spoons were brass 'and I tested them to find out and it
seemed so; some time afterwards as I came in from a
stroll with Mr. [afterwards Father] Purbrick he told
me Hügel [the late Baron Anatole von Hügel] had said
the scarlet and rose colour of flamingos was found to
be due to a fine copper powder on the feathers. As he

said this I tasted the brass in my mouth. It is what they call unconscious cerebration, a bad phrase.' There are magnificent descriptions of abbeys and cathedrals, elaborate criticisms of the pictures in Burlington House and the National Art Gallery that would have delighted Ruskin or Pater; and we have devoted a whole appendix to show what he thought of clouds. He visits the Houses of Lords and Commons and sees Mr. Gladstone 'preparing to speak and writing fast. . . . Lowe who sat next him, looked something like an apple in the snow!' As an intimate friend of Bernard Vaughan he meets the Bishop of Plymouth, 'my sixth Vaughan', and when Dr. Herbert Vaughan visits St. Beuno's he writes 'Greek Iambics for the reception academy'.

All this while Hopkins was pursuing the rigid course of studies demanded by the Society. But even in this he has an interesting avocation in the disciple-ship of Duns Scotus.[1] In the Isle of Man he had 'begun to get hold of the copy of Scotus on the Sentences in the Badely Library and was flush with a new stroke of enthusiasm. It may come to nothing or it may be a mercy from God. But just then when I took in any inscape of the sky or sea I thought of Scotus.' A year later he writes: 'I walked with Herbert Lucas by the river and talked Scotism with him for the last time.' And again, later: 'I met Mr. David Lewis a great Scotist and at the same time old Mr. Brande Morris was making a retreat with us; so that oddly enough I made the acquaintance with two, and I suppose the only two, Scotists in England in one week.' This

---

[1] Cf. G. M. H.'s sonnet: 'Duns Scotus's Oxford'.

avocation for Scotism eventually became a passion
with him (despite the fact that Jesuit theologians are
Thomistic), so that he was often embroiled in minor
duels of intellect. However, he completed a successful
course of theology at St. Beuno's and left there with
the reputation of being one of the best moral theologians among his contemporaries.

One of his contemporaries writes:

My knowledge of Father Gerard Hopkins was
almost entirely confined to the time when we were
studying theology together at St. Beuno's. I shall
always have a grateful and affectionate remembrance
of him. . . . What struck me most of all in him was
his child-like guilelessness and simplicity, his gentle-
ness, tender-heartedness, and his loving compassion
for the young, the weak, the poor, and all who were
in any trouble or distress. Joined to this and closely
connected with it, was his purity of heart and shrink-
ing dread of anything that tended to endanger,
especially in the young, the angelic virtue.

Of his ability I need scarcely speak. He had a
distinct dash of genius. His opinion on any subject
in Heaven and earth was always worth listening to
and always fresh and original. . . . He was also most
sensitive and this caused him to suffer much. I have
rarely known any one who sacrificed so much in
undertaking the yoke of religion. If I had known
him outside, I should have said that his love of
speculation and originality of thought would make
it almost impossible for him to submit his intellect to
authority.

Another who knew Gerard at this time wrote:

His mind was of too delicate a texture to grapple
with the rough elements of human life, but his kindness of heart and unselfishness showed themselves
in a thousand different ways, that gave full expression to the old words: 'Nil humani a me alienum
puto'. The high order of his intellect was at once
made evident to all who came into serious contact
with him. True it was of a somewhat unpractical
turn, but the various and often amusing extravagances into which it was from time to time in con-
sequence beguiled, only added another point of
attractiveness to his character. The result of all was
a man so loveable that we shall not soon look upon
his like again.

From St. Beuno's he went to Farm Street Church
in London as select preacher, and thence to Oxford,[1]
and finally to Liverpool. His sermon notes are, for
the most part, simple, direct, and, as usual, filled with
interesting originality. It was this last quality which
drew from his superiors the recommendation to write
out each sermon before delivering it; but it must be
confessed that poor Gerard seldom preached the same
sermon he had faithfully prepared! His sermons,
however, manifest a thorough knowledge of the Old
and New Testament and the Fathers. Like Bossuet,
he begins by stating the plan of the sermon. The

[1] Baron de Paravicini, an undergraduate friend of G. M. H. when the
latter was at Balliol, erected a holy water font in St. Aloysius Church,
Oxford, with the following inscription: 'In memory of Father Gerard
Hopkins, S.J., who died June 8, 1889. R.I.P. Sometime priest of this
Mission. Formerly of Balliol College.'

following (a conclusion of a sermon on original sin) is a fair example of his style:

> She fell, but still God's Kingdom was not fallen yet, because it turned upon the man's obedience not the woman's. Then came the meeting between husband and wife and she learnt that she was deceived and undone. Then her husband must share her lot for better and worse ; this selfish and fallen woman would drag her husband in her fall, and as she had had no thought of God's honour in her innocence, so in her sin she had no charity for her husband. She had so little love for him that she said if he loved her he must share her lot. Most dearly he loved her, and she stood before him now lovely and her beauty heightened by distress, a thing never seen before in Paradise, herself a Tree of Knowledge of Good and Evil and offering him its fruit; herself a Tree of Life, the mother of all flesh to be. He listened to her voice. He left his Heavenly Father and clave to his wife and they two were in one fallen flesh; for he took the stolen goods, and harboured the forfeit person of the thief, rebelling against God, the world's great landlord, owner of earth and man, who had bestowed upon him Paradise, who had bestowed upon him the body of his wife; for her he ate the fatal fruit, making a new contract, a new commonwealth with Eve alone, and rebelling against God his law-giver and judge. With that the contract with God was broken, the commonwealth undone, the kingdom divided and brought to desolation. God was left upon His throne but His subject

had deserted to the enemy, God was left with His rights but His tenant had refused Him payment, God was left a father but His children were turned to children of wrath. Then followed the disinheriting of the disobedient son. Then followed the first and most terrible of evictions, when Cherubim swayed the fiery sword and man was turned from Paradise; then followed the judgement of death and the execution of the sentence which we feel yet. . . .

At this point we may pause to note some faint adumbrations of Hopkins's spiritual life as a Jesuit. It will be remembered that the diaries begun at Oxford were ever afterwards continued, but where he had used the same book prior to 1868 for all his entries, he subsequently used two, one for spiritual phenomena, the other for intellectual. The first he destroyed. The second remains, and is occasionally hallowed by a note not in keeping with its original purpose. Thus, for instance, he writes in 1868:

> One day in the Long Retreat (which ended on Christmas Day) they were reading in the refectory Sister Emmerich's account of the Agony in the Garden and I suddenly began to cry and sob and could not stop. I put it down for this reason, that if I had been asked a minute beforehand I should have said nothing of the sort was going to happen and even if it did I stood in a manner wondering at myself not seeing in my reason the traces of an adequate cause for such strong emotion—and traces of it, I say, because of course the cause in itself is adequate for the sorrow of a lifetime. I remember much the same

thing on Maundy Thursday, when the presanctified Host was carried to the Sacristy. But neither the weight nor the stress of sorrow (that is to say of the thing which should cause sorrow) by themselves move us or bring the tears; as a sharp knife does not cut for being pressed as long as it is pressed without any shaking of the hand, but there is always one touch, something striking sideways and unlooked for, which in both cases undoes resistance and pierces; and this may be so delicate that the pathos seems to have gone directly to the body and cleared the understanding in its passage. On the other hand, the pathetic touch by itself, as in dramatic pathos, will only draw slight tears if its matter is not important or not of import to us, the strong emotion coming from a force which was gathered before it was discharged: in this way a knife may pierce the flesh which it had happened only to graze and only grazing will go no deeper.

[1869] A penance which I was doing from Jan. 25 to July 25 prevented my seeing much that half year.

[1870] I do not think I have ever seen anything more beautiful than the blue-bell I have been looking at. I know the beauty of Our Lord by it. Its inscape is mixed of strength and grace, like an ash-tree. The head is strongly drawn over backwards and arched down like a cutwater drawing itself back from the line of the keel. The lines of the bell strike and overlie this, rayed but not symmetrically, some lie parallel. They looked steely against the paper, the shades lying between the bells and behind the cockled petal-ends and nursing up the precision of their distinctness, the petal-ends themselves being delicately lit. Then there is the straightness of the trumpets in the bells softened by the slight entasis and by the square splay of the mouth. One bell, the lowest, some way detached and carried on a longer footstalk, touched out with the lips of the petals. . . .

[13 March 1872] After a time of trial and especially a morning in which I did not know which way to turn, as the account of de Rance's final conversion was being read at dinner, the verse *Qui confidunt in Domino sicut Mons Sion,* which satisfied him and resolved him to enter his abbey of La Trappe, by the mercy of God came strongly home to me too, so that I was choked for a little while and could not keep in my tears.

[30 Aug.–8 Sept. 1873] Retreat, of which there are notes in my meditation papers. I received as I think a great mercy about Dolben.

[18 Sept. 1873] I had a nightmare that night. I thought something or some one leapt onto me and held me quite fast: this I think woke me, so that after this I shall have had the use of reason. . . . I had lost all muscular stress, but not sensitive, feeling where each limb lay and thinking that I could recover myself if I could move my finger and then the arm and so the whole body. The feeling is terrible: the body no longer swayed as a piece by the nervous and muscular instress seems to fall in, and hang like a dead weight on the chest. I cried on the Holy Name and by degrees recovered myself as I thought to do.

[1874] Our Schools at Roehampton ended with two days of examination before St. Ignatius' feast— the 31st [of July]. I was very tired, seemed deeply cast down, till I had some kind words from the Provincial. . . . The tax on my strength has been greater than I have felt before: at least now at Teignmouth I feel myself weak and can do but little. But in all this Our Lord goes His own way.

[17 Aug. 1874] We went over to Ugbrooke at Lord Clifford's invitation. . . . As we drove home the stars came out thick: I leant back to look at them and my heart opening more than usual praised our Lord to and in whom all that beauty comes home.

[6 Sept. 1874] . . . Looking all round but most in looking far up the valley I felt an instress and charm of Wales. Indeed in coming here I began to feel a desire to do something for the conversion of Wales. I began to learn Welsh too but not with very pure intentions perhaps . . . and so I saw that I must give it up. And at that time I was very bitterly feeling the weariness of life and shed many tears, perhaps not wholly into the breast of God, but with some unmanliness in them too, and sighed and panted to Him.

[10 Sept. 1874] At night the retreat began, given by Fr. Coleridge. There are some remarks on it in my notes of meditation.

[20 Sept. 1874] Ordination of priests—sixteen, including many Germans from Ditton. At the singing of the *Veni Creator* and giving of the Orders I was by God's mercy deeply touched.

In 1884 came to Hopkins the most important appointment of his life which sent him to lecture in the chair of Greek at the then Royal University of Ireland. Jowett had called him the star of Balliol and said that he was one of the finest Greek scholars he had ever seen at Balliol, all of which made the Senate of the University extremely desirous to secure his services. Newman had already breathed upon the waters of higher education in Ireland, and had made the Catholic University forever famous by his 'Idea of a University'. Over a quarter of a century had passed since Newman's removal from Dublin and over all hung the lowering clouds of failure. The Society had manned the sinking ship and to the staunch old converts from Oxford, Arnold and Ormsby, added youthful converts and Oxonians, Fathers Darlington and Browne, all of whom, like Hopkins, had come under the direct sway of Newman's influence. Father Thomas Finley, also a convert, was taken from the Rectorship of Belvedere College to a Fellowship at the University, and with him were Curtis 'the exquisite mathematician whom Hopkins insisted must number a hare in his Darwinian ancestry, and O'Carroll, who could pray to each Apostle in a different tongue'. Over all were Dr. Delaney, President of University College and Senator of the Royal University, and Monsignor Molloy its gifted Rector.

Into this assemblage of choice spirits came Hopkins as a worthy complement. The conditions were trying on account of the national indifference to the Royal University, but his work itself was interesting and consoling, and his friends congenial and satisfying; then too, the monotony of routine was easily broken by the utmost freedom he had received from his superiors. It is necessary to insist on this because so many writers have drawn tragic portraits of an exiled Englishman slowly dying of loneliness, drudgery, and despair. Nothing could be more foreign to the sincere and candid accounts of those who lived with him. We may discern a triple sorrow which descended on the shoulders of Hopkins, but it did not in any degree eclipse his peace and happiness.

The first sorrow, or inconvenience, sprang from the labours of a semi-annual examination of candidates. Hopkins was never a man of practical affairs (though he had successfully filled the office of Minister—or Bursar—at Mount St. Mary's College, Chesterfield), and when the board were crying for the returns, they found poor Gerard, at three a.m., his head swathed in wet towels, harassed with scruples at the award or non-award of half-marks! But to imagine that a few weeks of distasteful work darkened his whole life is manifestly absurd.

The second sorrow sprang from the political atmosphere in which he lived. Of this Father Darlington who knew him intimately writes: 'It has been rumoured that he was unhappy in Ireland. This is not the case.... Politics never upset his equilibrium to make him unhappy.' However, he did resent anything that in any way touched the honour of the 'land that bred me', and one remembers Newman's answer to Hopkins's anxiety about 'Irish rebels'. The two following birthday letters from Hopkins to Newman betray his mind in these matters; they both were written from University College, Dublin, the first on 20 February 1884:

YOUR EMINENCE AND DEAREST FATHER, PAX CHRISTI.

I wish you a very bright tomorrow and health and happiness and the abundance of God's grace for the ensuing year.

I am writing from where I never thought to be, in a University for Catholic Ireland begun under your leadership, which has since those days indeed long and unhappily languished, but for which we now—with God's help—hope a continuation or restoration of success. In the events which have brought me here I recognize the hand of providence, but nevertheless have felt and feel an unfitness which led me at first to try to decline the offer made me and now does not allow my spirits to rise to the level of the position and its duties. But perhaps the things of most promise with God begin with weakness and fear.

These buildings since you knew them have fallen into a deep dilapidation. They were a sort of wreck or ruin when our Fathers some months since came in, and the costly last century ornamentation of flutes and festoons and muses on the walls is still much in contrast with the dinginess and dismantlement all round. Only one thing looks bright, and that no longer belongs to the college, the little church of your building, the Byzantine style of which reminds me of the Oratory and bears your impress clearly enough.

I should have said in the beginning that I am to

convey from Fr. Delaney the best wishes of all the College, together with my own.

I remain your Eminence's affectionate son in Christ,

GERARD M. HOPKINS, S.J.

Four years later Hopkins wrote:

. . . I wish you a very happy eighty-eighth birthday and year and as many more as God shall send. It seems that you still enjoy the blessings granted Moses.

This poor University College, the somehow-or-other-manned wreck of the Catholic University is afloat and not sinking; rather making a very little way than losing any. There is scarcely any public interest in the University question. Nay, there is none. But this does not prevent good and really patriotic people in a quiet, but not ineffective way, doing which can be done to advance it.

Politically, the times are most troubled. I live, I may say, in an air most painful to breathe and this comes home to me more, not less, with time. There is to my mind only one break in the sky, but it is a notable one; it is from Rome. The Pope is acting very much as I thought he would and the effect of what he does, though slowly and guardedly, is likely to be powerful. . . .[1]

Of Hopkins's third sorrow it is more difficult to speak. It sprang from causes which have their origin

---

[1] Father Darlington tells me an interesting anecdote of how when the Royal University was conferring a degree on Father Perry the astronomer, they sang a nationalist song. G. M. H. rose and went away. ' "You know", he said to me next day, "I would not have done that if it hadn't been so wicked!" '

in true mysticism. Hopkins, smiling and joyful with his friends, was at the same time on the bleak heights of spiritual night with his God. All writers on mysticism—St. Teresa, St. John of the Cross, Poulain, Maumigny, &c.—have told us that this severe trial is the greatest and most cherished *gift* from One Who has accepted literally His servant's oblation. Hopkins was always remembered by all who met him as essentially a priest, a deep and prayerful religious. With the fine uncompromising courage of his initial conversion, he pursued his never-ending quest after spiritual perfection. The celebrated 'terrible' sonnets are only terrible in the same way that the beauty of Jesus Christ is terrible. Only the strong pinions of an eagle can realize the cherished happiness of such suffering. It is a place where Golgotha and Thabor meet. Read in this light his poems cease to be tragic.

Death came to Gerard Hopkins in the fifth year of his sojourn in Ireland. The last years of his life may be best told in the words of one of his most intimate friends:

I saw a good deal of Father Gerard Hopkins during the last two or three years of his life; but as I was an invalid, unable to leave my couch all that time, I had no knowledge of the incidents of his daily life beyond what I heard from himself or from our common friends.

He came to Dublin from Stonyhurst in 1884, on his appointment to a fellowship in the Royal University. I have heard from Lord Emly, the Vice-Chancellor of the University, that the recommendatory letters presented when he sought election, spoke so highly of his character and attainments (especially one from Dr. Jowett, the Master of Balliol, in praise of his scholarship), as to make the Senate most anxious to obtain his services; and Lord Emly at the same time expressed—what is the universal feeling among that body—the loss the University has sustained by his death.

His duties consisted in teaching Latin and Greek in the Catholic University College—where he resided—and in examining in classics for the various degrees of the Royal University. The first of these duties he liked, taking much interest in his pupils; but he had a great repugnance to the labour and responsibility involved in the preparation of the examination papers, and in subsequently correcting and awarding them marks. Nevertheless, in his scrupulous anxiety to be just and fair, he was accustomed to give to these tasks a far greater amount of care and time than most conscientious examiners would have considered necessary.

He occupied his spare hours, which were not many, in literary work. He had collected and put together with a view to publication in some work on British dialects, the idioms of the different Irish provinces. He wrote several articles for the *Classical Review*. He was engaged at the time of his death upon a critical work dealing with difficult passages in the plays of Aristophanes, the true meaning of which he believed that he had discovered. [1] He read

---

[1] We learn from Patmore's letters that he was also engaged on a critical work on Homer.

a great deal of general literature, considering the little leisure time he had, but I have heard him say that he could get on quite happily with no other book than his Breviary. He was very fond of music and composed 'fugues', which were much admired by Sir Robert Stewart, Mus.Doc.

On everything that he wrote and said there was the stamp of originality, and he had the keenest appreciation of humour. I think the characteristics in him that most struck and edified all of us who knew him were, first, what I should call his priestly spirit; this showed itself not only in the reverential way he performed his sacred duties, and spoke on sacred subjects, but in his whole conduct and conversation; and secondly, his devotion and loyalty to the Society of Jesus.

During the few years of which I speak, he was very seldom away from home, having a notion that he ought not to take a holiday unless his health required it. He passed one Christmas with his friend, Mr. Cassidy, of Monastereven. In the summer of 1888, he went for a brief trip to Scotland with the Rev. Robert Curtis, S.J., and occasionally he came to stay for a few days at Judge O'Hagan's country house at Howth where I spent two summers. He was of a very retiring disposition and made few acquaintances in Dublin, even these he seldom visited, and very rarely could he be induced to ask permission to lunch or dine out. Without permission he could scarcely be prevailed on to take a cup of tea. Speaking of his strictness in this particular, reminds me of a pun of his which may be worth repeating. One day he had taken a long walk to a village some miles from Dublin. He called on the curate of the place, the Rev. Mr. Wade, who invited him to remain for dinner. He declined, saying that he hadn't leave. 'Oh! as to that', said Father Wade, 'I will take the whole responsibility on myself.' 'That's all very well,' replied Father Hopkins, 'you may be weighed (Wade) but I should be found wanting,' and he returned home.

A day or two after Low Sunday 1889 he fell ill of typhoid fever. From the outset he was fully alive to the gravity of his state, and, I believe, never shared the hope that others from time to time entertained, that he would pull through.

During the night of Wednesday, the 5th of June, a serious change for the worse took place in his condition, and when the doctors arrived early next morning, they pronounced his case well-nigh desperate. Father Wheeler, S.J., who attended him all through his illness with affectionate care, told him of his danger, and gave him the Holy Viaticum, which he received with the deepest devotion.

On hearing that his parents were coming from England, he appeared to dread their arrival, because of the pain it would give them to see him prostrate, but when the first interview was over, he expressed the happiness he felt at having them with him.

He quite realized that he was dying and asked each day for the Holy Viaticum. He received It for the last time on the morning of the day of his death, Saturday, the 8th of June.

The final blessing and absolution were also then

given him at his own request, and he was heard two or three times to say 'I am so happy, I am so happy'. Soon afterwards, he became too weak to speak, but he appeared to follow mentally the prayers for the dying, which were said a little before noon by Father Wheeler, and joined in by his parents. As the end approached he seemed to grow more collected, and retained consciousness almost up to the moment, half-past one o'clock, when he passed peacefully away. He was buried in the burial ground of the Society at Glasnevin. *Requiescat in Pace.*

APPENDIX I

BIOGRAPHICAL NOTE

1844. June 11, born at Stratford, Essex.
1852. Removal to Oak Hill, Hampstead.
1854. Attended Highgate School.
1855. Met M. Clarke at the Isle of Wight.
1857. Went for a tour through the Rhinelands.
1859. Wrote a Prize-poem: 'The Escorial'.
1860. Went for a tour through Southern Germany.
1862. Won a gold medal for Prize-poem: 'A Vision of Mermaids'.
1863. Won an Exhibition for Balliol College.
1866. Received into the Catholic Church.
1867. Took a Double-first in 'Greats'.
       Taught at the Oratory School, Birmingham.
1868. Went for a tour through Switzerland.
       Entered the Jesuit Novitiate, Roehampton.
1870. Philosophical studies at St. Mary's Hall, Stonyhurst.
1873. Taught Classics at Manresa House, Roehampton.
1874. Theological studies at St. Beuno's College, North Wales.
1877. Ordination to the Priesthood.
       Preacher at Farm Street Church, London.
       Sub-minister at Mount St. Mary's College, Chesterfield.
1878. Preacher at St. Aloysius Church, Oxford.
1879. Preacher at St. Francis Xavier's Church, Liverpool.
1881. Third Year Novitiate, Roehampton.
1882. Taught Classics at Stonyhurst.
1883. Went for a trip to Holland.
1884. Chair of Greek at the Royal University, Dublin.
1889. June 8, died.

APPENDIX II

JUVENILE PROSE EXTRACTS

IN presenting to the reader a character so fascinating and so original, it were better to have him emerge from his own writings where possible, rather than through mere external description, because the former method, for the most part, is dynamic and interesting, the latter, static and formidable. Gerard Hopkins is, above all, an elusive spirit, far too great for a short synthesis, and we are fortunate, indeed, in having some of his writings—private jottings which were never meant to see the light; the spirit in negligé, as it were—which, being written so naturally and so spontaneously, betray one aspect of the man in the best possible way.

His mind was so restless an inquirer, his sensibilities so finely tuned, that almost everything he wrote turned to fine gold.

If at any time that excessively well-thumbed phrase, 'le style c'est l'homme' were called in question, it could certainly be defended by our present subject, and if read in this light, his work will reward study. One cannot but recall a well-known passage of Pater which, illustrating the spirit of an age, illustrates also the spirit of Hopkins: 'one might think there had been no effort in it: that here was but the almost mechanical transcript of a time naturally intrinsically poetic, a time in which one could hardly have spoken at all without ideal effect, or the sailors pulled down their boat without making a picture in "the great style" against a sky charged with marvels.' Nowhere in the whole course of his life and writings does Gerard's mind cease to be 'naturally poetic', and the random notes we quote are as conclusive as are his more deliberate essays.

The present scene of his life is in Switzerland where Hopkins was looking upon those same sights which inspired men from the time of the great Halbsuter to the contemporary Airoldi or Ciocarri. We will quote at some length from his private diary:

July 19, 1868. . . . Walked up the valley of the Aar, sallow-coloured and torrent, to the Grimsel. The heights bounding the valley soon became a mingle of lilac and green, the first the colour of the rock, the other the grass crestings, and seemed to group above in crops and rounded buttresses, yet to be cut sharp in horizontal or leaning planes below. At a turn in the road the foam-cuffs in the river, looked down upon, were of the crispiest endive spraying. . . . At times the valley opened in cirques, amphitheatres, enclosing levels of plain, and the river then ran between flaky flat-fish isles made of cindery lily-white stones. In one place over a smooth table of rock came slipping down a blade of water looking like and as evenly crisped as fruitnets let drop and falling slack.

We saw Handeck waterfall. It is in fact the meeting of the two waters, the right the Aar sallow and jade-coloured, the left a smaller stream of clean lilac-foam. It is the greatest fall we have seen. The lower half is hidden in spray; I watched the great bushes of foam-water, the texture of branchings and water-spandrels which makes them up. At their outsides nearest the rock they gave off showers of drops strung together into little quills which sprang out in fans.

On crossing the Aar again there was as good a fall as some we have paid to see, all in jostling foam-bags.

Across the valley too we saw the fall of the Gelmer—like milk chasing round blocks of coal; or a girdle or long purse of white weighted with irregular black rubies, carelessly thrown aside and lying in jutty bends, with a black clasp of the same stone at the top.

July 20. Fine.

Walked down to the Rhone glacier. It has three stages—first, a smoothly-moulded bed in a pan or theatre of thorny peaks, swells of ice rising through the snow-sheet and the snow itself tossing and fretting into the sides of the rock walls in spray-like points: this is the first stage of the glaciers generally; it is like bright-plucked water swaying in a pail; second, after a slope nearly covered with landslips of moraine, was a ruck of horned waves steep and narrow: now in the upper Grindelwald glacier between the bed or highest stage was a descending limb which was like the rude and knotty bossings of a strombus shell;

third, the foot, a broad limb opening out and reaching the plain shaped like the fan-fin of a dolphin or a great bivalve shell turned on its face, the flutings in either case being suggested by the crevasses, and the ribs by the risings between them, these being swerved and inscaped strictly to the notion of the mass.

We went into the grotto and also the vault from which the Rhone flows. It looked like a blue tent and as you went further in changed to lilac. As you come out the daylight grazes the groins with gleaming rose-colour. The ice inside has a branchy wire texture. The man showed us the odd way in which a little piece of ice will stick against the walls—as if drawn by a magnet.

Standing on the glacier, saw the prismatic colours in the clouds, and worth saying what sort of clouds: it was fine shapeless skins of fretted make, full of eye-brows or like linings of curled leaves which one finds in sheltered corners of a wood.

I had a trudge over the glacier and a tumble over the side moraine, which was one landslip of limestone. It was neighboured however by not sweet smells and many flowers—small crimson pinks, and brown tulip-like flower we have seen so often, another which we first saw yesterday like Solomon's seal but rather coarser with a spike of greenish veiny-leaved blossom, &c.

We drove down the Rhone valley to Visp and soon entered a Catholic canton. The Churches here have those onion steeples nearly all, being in some cases newly covered in bright tin or lead. They enclose the head of the cross in a triangle very commonly: it looks like a beacon at sea.

Soon we saw the vines trellised—hemp swaying in its sweet-smelling thickset beds—that sprayed silvery weed something like tamarisk leaping over the road: what is it? Maize very high. Spanish chestnuts: their inscape bold, jutty, somewhat oak-like, attractive, the branching visible, and the leaved peaks spotted so as to make crests of eyes.

Plushy look and very rich warm green of mountain grass, noticed especially at the Rhone glacier.

In the valley a girl with spindle and distaff tending cows.

July 21. Bright.

We walked up the valley of the Visp to Zermatt, a beautiful valley and the river in torrent.

Vines, as I have often seen, like the fretting of pike-blades. Chalk, blue of cornflowers.

We lunched at St. Niclaus and shortly after leaving it saw the Little Matterhorn and the Breithorn closing the valley. The latter is like a broad piece of hacked or knocked flintstone—flint of the half-chalky sort, for the mountain is covered with snow, while the breaks of rock remind one of the dark eyes or spots in the white; and this resemblance did not disappear even at much nearer.

Tall larches by the river.

Coffee-foam waterfalls ran into the Visp, which above one of these being paler and becoming at the place a little smoother —for else it never for a hand's breadth could recover from one crumpled sheet of jolting foam—looked like a strew of waving poppy-leaf.

Note how river billows all look back. Not unapparent that the Matterhorn is like a Greek galley stranded, a reared-up rostrum—the sharp quains or arrêtes the gunwales, the deck of the forecastle looking upon Zermatt, the figure-head looking the other way, reaching up in the air, the cutwater and ram descending and abutting on a long reef, the gable-length of the mountain.

July 22.   Morning fine; in afternoon rain as we went up the Riffel; fine evening.

Up the Riffel, from which, the point of view somewhat changing, the Matterhorn looks like a sea-lion couchant or a sphinx, and again like the hooded-snake frontal worn by the Egyptian Kings. They range on the other side of Zermatt and skirting the Zermatt valley are concave, cusped; they run like waves in the wind, ricked, and sharply inscaped.[1]

[1] When transcribing these notes, so rich in imagery and so spontaneous, Gerard's description of the Matterhorn reminded me of Ruskin's which I had but lately re-read. Though Ruskin was conscious of an audience and Hopkins not, yet it may be of interest to quote Ruskin's here, to compare the different images the same object evoked.

'It has been falsely represented as a peak or a tower. It is a vast rigid promontary, connected at its western root with the Dent d'Erin, and lifting

The Monte Rosa range are dragged over with snow like cream. As we looked at them the sky behind them became dead purple, the effect unique; and then the snow according to its lie and its faces differenced itself, the upward-looking faces taking shade, the vertical light, like lovely damask. Above the Breithorn, Antares sparkled like a bright crab-apple tingling in the wind.

July 23.   Bright morning, thunderous afternoon. Up to the Gornergrat. It is the peculiarity of this view, the finest we saw, that the Monte Rosa range appeals to the eye solely by form, the sense of size disappearing, becoming irrelevant, and not rising in the mind. On the round-headed height which lies in front of the Jumeaux and on the Breithorn, both over-lipped with heavy cowls of snow, the glassy reflections within the shadow very noticeable, and in the Breithorn especially the wavings and impressions of these great lips or cornices crisply cut off below remind one of thatch-eaves and rows of little three-cornered drops, the beginnings of the long pleatings noticed before, of the gutter in the Doric entablature.

July 24.   Bright.

At sunset great bulks of brassy cloud hanging round, which changed their colour to bright reds over the sundown, and to fruit tree blossom colour opposite; later a honey-brown edged the Dent Blanche and Weisshorn ridge.

July 25.   But too bright.

Up at two to ascend the Breithorn. Stars twirling brilliantly, Taurus up, a pale light stressily edging the eastern skyline, and lightning mingled with the dawn. In the twilight we tumbled over the moraine and glacier until the sunrise brightly flushed the snow and then the colour changing through metallic shades of yellow recovered to white.

From the summit the view on the Italian side was broken by endless ranges of part-vertical dancing cloud, the highest and furthest flaked or foiled like fungus and coloured pink. Even

itself like a rearing horse with its face to the east. All the way along the flank of it, for half a day's journey on the Zmutt glacier, the grim black terraces of its foundations range almost without a break.'   *The Stones of Venice.*

with one companion ecstacy is almost banished: you want to be alone and to feel that, and leisure—all pressure taken off.

The valley is beautiful. The mountains bounding it give one more the impression of height than I have seen in any other valley—I was noticing on each side of a buttress of rock two fan-shaped slant tables of green, flush with one another and laced over with a *plant* or root-work of zigzag brooks ravelled out and shining.

July 26. Sunday. There was no church nearer than Valtournanches, but there was to be mass said in a little chapel for the guides going up to Tyndal at two o'clock in the morning, and so I got up for this, my burnt face in a dreadful state and running. We went down with lanterns. It was an odd scene: two of the guides or porters served; the noise of the torrent outside accompanied the priest. Then to bed again.

Day fine. We did not get a completely clear view of the Matterhorn from this side.

In the afternoon we walked down the valley, which is beautiful, to Valtournanches. We passed a gorge at the end of which it was curious to see a tree rubbing and ruffling with the water at the neck just above a fall. Then we saw a grotto, that is deep and partly covered chambers of rock through which the torrent river runs—a little beyond was a wayside chapel with a woman kneeling at a window a long time. Further, across the valley a pretty village, the houses white, deep-eaved, pierced with small square windows at effective distances, and crossed with balconies, and above, a grove of ash or sycamore, or both, sprayed all one way, like water-weed beds in a running stream, very English-looking. Beyond again, in the midst of a slope of meadow slightly pulled like an unsteady and swelling surface of water, some ashes growing in a beautifully clustered 'bouquet', the inward bend of the left-hand stem being partly real, partly apparent, and helped by τύχη τέχνην στερχούσῃ—dim mountains down the valley red in the sunset.

July 27. Walked down the valley to Chatillon, the road soon passing through pleasant groves of Spanish chestnut full of great scattered rocks. From Chatillon, where I felt ill, we drove up the valley of the Doise to Aosta and I saw very little of it.

July 28. First fine; then on the road a thunderstorm with hard rain, the thunder musical and like gongs and rolling in great floors of sound.

We drove to St. Remy. As we approached it the hills 'fledged' with larches which hung in them shaft after shaft like green-feathered arrows.

Noticed also the cornfields below us laid by the rain in curls like a lion's mane—very impressive. We walked on to the St. Bernard's Hospice.[1]

July 29. From Martigny we took the train to Vevey. In the train I was noticing that strange rotten-wovey cloud which shapes in leaf over leaf of wavy or eyebrow texture: it is like fine webs or gossamers held down by many invisible threads on the undersides against a wind which between these points kept blowing them up into balls. The curious rottenness about them reminds one of that dark green silken oozy sea-weed with holes in it which lines and hangs from piers and slubbered wood in the sea. This case was a well-pronounced one.

Later in the plain of the Rhone approaching the lake, white-rose clouds formed the ground of the sky, near the sundown taking straight ranks and gilded by the light; in front heavy dark masses with their edges soaked red and fragments of bright thread. At Vevey there was dancing in the salle à manger of the Trois Couronnes and the moon outside was roughing the lake to silver and dinting and tooling it with sparkling holes.

July 30. Morning grey: soft braided clouds overhanging the lake, which was dim; fine afternoon and evening.

By steamer to Geneva.

July 31. Fine. The lake sharp dark blue from the shore.

In morning to see the cathedral, which is remarkable for the great beauty of the capitals, especially their abacuses; and mouldings too of two arches near the door were very beautiful and elaborate and wanted long study, which I could not give. . . .

In the afternoon we took train for Paris and passed through a country of pale grey rocky hills of a strong and simple outscape covered with fields of waving green vines.

---

[1] I have omitted his description of the Hospice, as unnecessarily lengthening this already long quotation.

August 1. Through Paris to Dieppe and by Newhaven home. Day—bright. Sea calm, with little walking wavelets edged with fine eyebrow crispings, and later nothing but a matting or chain-work on the surface, and even that went, so that the smoothness was marbly and perfect, and, between the just-corded near-sides of the waves, rising like fishes' backs and breaking with darker blue the pale blue of the general field; in the very sleek hollows, came out golden crumbs of reflections from the chalk cliffs. Peach-coloured sundown and above some simple gilded masses of cloud, which later became finer, smaller, and scattering all away.

August 24. Fresh and mostly fine—baggy cob-web clouds sometimes overcasting the sky.

Walked to St. Alban's with Baillie and back by train. The country is very green and set with good trees. The abbey is, I suppose the least injured in England. It stands high, with a great massive Norman tower now empoverished in look by brown plaster, in which the tympanes of the highest window-arches—otherwise flush and blind: the tympanes I mean—are pierced oddly with three-cornered pigeon-holes. The nave is very long, the roof, third-pointed, very low, invisible in fact, except at the end. The nave divides itself accidentally at the points where the work of conversion of style began or ended: thus on the south side all the Norman work is converted—in the clearstory the western part to First, the eastern to Second Pointed; the triforium I forget: the aisle windows are wide and well traceried but small; below these are the blind traceried arches of the inner side of the cloisters (not now standing)—these last and some windows in the antechapel to the east between the church and the lady-chapel are beautiful and in the purest style—on the N. side the clearstory is in the western part converted to First Pointed, the rest remains Norman; the rest I forget. None of this side has any Middle Pointed. The outside on the whole is plain and, where Norman, barbarous. The great number of the clearstory windows gives it character and beauty. Inside the whitewash has been cleared and the carving is fresh to a degree, the stone, which comes from not far off, being when covered from the weather durable though soft. The conversion

is very perceptible inside. In the depth of the round arches has
been laid bare some simple and broad diaper painting (chequers,
stripes, &c.) and on piers on the western side of the pillars
(above altars now gone from their places) frescoes of the Cruci-
fixion—the same subject differently treated in each—and, below,
sometimes, other subjects. Note that one of the crosses was a
tree, as at Godshill, Isle of Wight. The cieling[1] with its old
painting is complete from end to end; that of the choir was
Middle Pointed and the effect of the slant stripes on the ribs of
the groining, specially where they met, was noticeable. The
Third-Pointed altar-screen, especially behind, and the choir
screen of the same character were beautiful in design and pro-
portion. So also are two chantries, one on the N. side of the
high altar, the other Duke Humphrey's on the S. behind. The
abbot's passage so-called is remarkable for the curious astragalous
moulding of the interlaced wall-tracery. There is a little Saxon
work, like rude turning in carpentry, merely barbarous. The
building is mostly of tiles taken from the Roman walls of Veru-
lam. It is perhaps worth noticing that the little curled ends of
some corbels in the nave are freakishly turned each a different
way.

August 30. Grey till past four: then fine.

I saw the phenomenon of the sheep flock on the downs again
from Croham Hurst. It ran like the water-packets on a leaf—
that collectively, but a number of globules so filmed over that
they would not flush together is the exacter comparison: at a
gap in the hedge they were huddled and shaking open as they
passed outwards they behaved as the drops would do (or a hand-
ful of shot) in reaching the brow of a rising and running over.

September 1. Fine.

To Ely. Noticed on the way that the E. counties trees are
upright in character, not squat. The country more burnt than
at Hampstead.

In the cathedral the great Norman tower is fine in effect;
otherwise the Norman work (transitional) is not striking, but
some of the foliate trailing on the capitals &c. remains and has

---

[1] Probably this spelling was intentional since the word ceiling is from
the French noun 'ciel'.

been repainted: it is in fact the loss of this correction that makes the style heavy and barbarous. The First-Pointed work has not much that is very good unless the large and taper corbels in the choir, some of them ribbed with long slant stems alternately leaved wound across them. The Flowing work is the middle interest of the building. In this the lantern and three bays of the choir eastwards, of Alan of Walsingham's work (1322 sqq.), are original, imaginative, and graceful, strict beauty being almost forbidden by the excess of the climacteric. The most striking points in this are the open-traceried arches of the triforium in the choir; the scroll of open tracery between the choir and the octagon arches, the flight or spirit in which it is impossible not to feel; the triplets of candle-flame-shaped canopies over brackets (now dismounted of their figures) above the lower arches in cross or lesser sides of the octagon; and most of all perhaps the pierced hoods formed by a blunter arch springing from the same points as the acuter one which encloses the great windows in these same cross sides and so cutting off the upper part of their tracery; the quasi fleur-de-lys tracery in these hoods is very happy. The nave is not very interesting but it is skilfully and successfully designed so as to concentrate and enclose the view up to the choir and not through width and scattering in the side arches let it lose or escape. The cieling of the nave painted by L'Estrange and after his death by Parry is con- tributively speaking effective, and quiet and good in colour, but the design is babyishly archaic. But even this suck-a-thumb is not so bad as the modern brasses and the window with the queen in her coronation robes and the bachelor and under- graduate and butler and bedmaker. The transept roof is painted and long angels with scarlet wings (original?) support the principals. The Lady-chapel (1321 sqq.) has its walls bordered all round with an ogee-canopied arcade of great richness, but the E. and W. windows, are strangely clumsy. The all-power- fulness of instress in mode and the immediateness of its effect are very remarkable.

APPENDIX III

PROSE EXTRACTS ON CLOUDS

Pas un atome de matière qui ne contienne pas la poésie.
FLAUBERT.

IN the previous appendix the juvenile prose of Gerard Hopkins was considered as a complement to the facts of his early life. Of itself it was of no very high value, but it may serve as a prelude to the following which, in certain respects, may well rank among the very great examples of the power of English Prose. Being but brief notes, they have not that prose-rhythm which would invigorate a public essay, but in nuances of form, nicety of expression, subtlety of impression, they are a miracle of artistic handicraft. They were begun in 1868 and were continued throughout the rest of his life, and it is interesting to note the gradual growth in his further mastery of expression. It seems strange, too, that though his 'silk-sack clouds' and 'skies of couple-colour as a brinded cow' do not share any remarkable or undue preponderance in his poems, yet they are almost ever-present in his prose. Their fidelity to objective truth reminds one of another poet—Tennyson—who also noted down his observations of natural phenomena; but apart from identity of purpose, the notes of the latter do not gain by any comparison, however lenient. Hopkins's notes seem to be a happy combination of the artistic powers of, say, Reynolds, with the command of Pater or of Ruskin—a rare occurrence—so that one would wish Hopkins had turned his talents to prose as well as verse.

The other evening after a very bright day, the air rinsed quite clear, there was a slash of glowing yolk-coloured sunset. On the first frost all day (which otherwise I do not remember for a long time), the air shining, but with vapour, the dead leaves frilled, the Park grass white with hoarfrost mixed with purple shadow. To-day—another clear afternoon with tender clouding after rain—one notices the crisp flat darkness of the woods against the sun and the smoky bloom they have opposite it. The trees budded and their sprays curled as if dressed for spring.

A few days before September 25 a fine sunrise seen from No.1, the upstairs bedroom—long skeins of meshy grey cloud a little ruddled underneath, not quite level but aslant, rising from left to right, and down on the left one more solid balk or bolt than the rest with a high-blown crest of flix or fleece above it.

About the same time a fine sunset which, looked at also from the upstairs windows, cut out the yews all down the approach to the house in bright flat pieces like wings in a theatre (as once before I noticed at sunrise from Magdalen tower), each shaped by its own sharp-cut shadow falling on the yew-tree next behind it, since they run E. and W. Westward under the sun the heights and groves in Richmond Park looked like dusty velvet being all flushed into a piece by the thick hoary golden light which slanted towards me over them.

Crossing the Common October 13 a fine sunset—great gold field; along the earth-line a train of dark clouds of knopped or clustery make pitching over at the top the way they were going; higher a slanting race of tapered or else coiling fish-like flakes such as are often seen; the gold etched with brighter gold and shaped in sandy pieces and looped and waved all in waterings: what more I have forgotten.

On the Common the snow was channelled all in parallels by the sharp driving wind and upon the tufts of grass (where by the dark colour showing through it looked greyish) it came to turret-like clusters or like broken shafts of basalt. In the Park in the afternoon the wind was driving little clouds of snow-dust which caught the sun as they rose and delightfully took the eyes; flying up the slopes they looked like breaks of sunlight fallen through ravelled cloud upon the hills and again like deep flossy velvet blown to the root by breath which passed all along. Nearer at hand along the road it was gliding over the ground in white wisps that between trailing and flying shifted and wimpled like so many silvery worms to and from one another.

March 12. A fine sunset: the higher sky dead clear blue bridged by a broad slant causeway rising from right to left of wisped or grass cloud, the wisps lying across; the sundown

yellow, moist with light but ending at the top in a foam of delicate white pearling and spotted with big tufts of cloud in colour
russet between brown and purple but edged with brassy light.
But what I note it all for is this: before I had always taken the
sunset and the sun as quite out of gauge with each other, as
indeed physically they are, for the eye after looking at the sun is
blunted to everything else and if you look at the rest of the sunset you must cover the sun, but to-day I inscaped them together
and made the sun the true eye and ace of the whole, as it is. It
was all active and tossing out light and started as strongly forward from the field as a long stone or a boss is the knob of the
chalice-stem: it is indeed by stalling it so that it falls into scape
with the sky.

The next morning a heavy fall of snow. It tufted and toed
the firs and yews and went on to load them till they were taxed
beyond their spring. The limes, elms, and Turkey-oaks it
crisped beautifully as with young leaf. Looking at the elms from
underneath you saw every wave in every twig (become by this
the wire-like stem to a finger of snow) and to the hangers and
flying sprays it restored, to the eye, the inscapes they had lost.
They were beautifully brought out against the sky, which was
on one side dead blue, on the other washed with gold.

At sunset the sun a crimson fire-ball, above one or two knots
of rosy cloud riddled with purple. After that, frost for two days.

September 24. First saw the Northern Lights. My eye was
caught by beams of light and dark very like the crown of horny
rays the sun makes behind a cloud. At first I thought of silvery
cloud until I saw that these were more luminous and did not dim
the clearness of the stars in the Bear. They rose slightly
radiating thrown out from the earth line. Then I saw soft pulses
of light one after another rise and pass upwards arched in shape
but waveringly and with the arch broken. They seemed to float,
not following the warp of the sphere as falling stars look to do
but free though concentrical with it. This busy working of
nature, wholly independent of the earth and seeming to go on
in a strain of time not reckoned by our reckoning of days and
years but simpler and as if correcting the preoccupation of the
world by being preoccupied with and appealing to and dated to,

M

the day of judgement was like a new witness to God and filled me with delightful fear.

October 25 (1870). A little before seven in the evening a wonderful Aurora; the same that was seen at Rome (shortly after its seizure by the Italian government) and taken as a sign of God's anger. It gathered a little below the zenith, to the SE. I think—a knot or crown, not a true circle, of dull blood-coloured horns and dropped long red beams down the sky on every side, each impaling its lot of stars. An hour or so later its colour was gone but there was still a pale crown in the same place: the skies were then clear and ashy and fresh with stars and there were flashes of or like sheet-lightning. The day had been very bright and clear, distances smart, herds of towering pillow clouds, one great stack in particular over Pendle was knoppled all in fine snowy tufts and pencilled with bloom-shadow of the greatest delicacy. In the sunset all was big and there was a world of swollen cloud holding the yellow-rose light like a lamp while a few sad milky-blue slips passed below it. At night violent hail-storms and hail again next day, and a solar halo. Worth noticing too perhaps the water-runs were then mulled and less beautiful than usual.

March 14. Bright morning, pied skies, hail! In the after-noon the wind was from the north, very cold; long bows of soft grey cloud straining the whole heaven but spanning the sky line with a slow entasis which left a strip of cold porcelain blue. The long ribs or girders were as rollers across the wind, not in it, but across them there lay fine grass-ends, sided off down the perspective, as if locks of vapour, blown free from the main ribs down the wind. Next day and next snow. Then in walking I saw the water-runs in the sand of unusual delicacy and the broken blots of snow in the dead bents of the hedge-banks I could find a square scaping in which helped the eye over another hitherto disordered field of things. (And if you look well at big pack-clouds overhead you will soon find a strong large quain-ing and squaring in them which makes each pack impressive and whole.) Pendle was beautiful: the face of snow on it and the tracks or galleys which streaked and parted this well-shaped out its roundness and boss and marked the slow tune of its long shoulder. One time it lay above a near hill of green field which, with the lands in it lined and plated by snow, was striped like a zebra: this Pendle repeated finer and dimmer.

Bright afternoon; clear distances; Pendle dappled with tufted shadow; west wind; interesting clouding, flat and lying in the warp of the heaven but the pieces with rounded outline and dolphin-backs showing in places and all was at odds and at L's, one piece with another. Later beautifully delicate crisping.

April 21. We have had other such afternoons, one to-day: the sky a beautiful grained blue, silky lingering clouds in flat-bottomed loaves, others a little browner in ropes or in burly-shouldered ridges swanny and lustrous, more in the zenith stray packs of a sort of violet paleness. White-rose cloud formed fast, not in the same density—some caked and swimming in a wan whiteness, the rest soaked with the blue and like the leaf of a flower held against the light and diapered out by the worm or veining of deeper blue, between rosette and rosette. Later moulding, which brought rain: in perspective it was vaulted in very regular ribs with fretting between; but these are not ribs; they are 'wracking' install made of these two realities—the frets, which are scarves of rotten cloud bellying upwards and drooping at their ends, and shaded darkest at the brow or tropic where they double to the eye, and the whiter field of sky showing between: the illusion looking down the 'waggon' is complete. These swaths of fretted cloud move in rank, not in file.

April 22. But such a lovely damasking in the sky as to-day I never felt before. The blue was charged with simple instress, the higher, zenith sky earnest and frowning, lower more light and sweet. High up again, breathing through woolly coats of cloud or on the quains and branches of the flying pieces it was the true exchange of crimson, nearer the earth, against the sun, it was turquoise, and in the opposite south-western bay below the sun it was like clear oil but just as full of colour, shaken over with slanted flashing 'travellers', all in flight, stepping one be-hind the other, their edges tossed with bright ravelling, as if white napkins were thrown up in the sun but not quite at the same moment so that they were all in a scale down the air falling one after the other to the ground.

It was a glowing yellow sunset. Pendle and all the hills rinsed clear, their heights drawn with a brimming light, in which windows or anything that could catch fluttered and laughed with the blaze—all bounded by the taut outline of a mealy blue shadow covering the valley, which was moist and giving up mist. Now where a strong shadow lay in a slack between two brows of Pendle appeared above the hill the same phenomenon I had seen twice before (once near Brussels`, a wedge of light faintly edged, green on the right side, red on the right, as a rainbow would be, leaning to the right and skirting the brow of the hill with a glowing edge. It lasted as long as I looked without change—I do not know how long but between five minutes and a quarter of an hour perhaps. It had clouds it seemed to me *behind* it. Later when it was growing dark and the glow of the sunset was quite gone I noticed to the right of the spot a little over Whalley—a rack of red cloud floating away, the red being I am persuaded a native colour, in fact it could not have been borrowed, the sun having long set and the higher clouds behind it not having it.

July ?. At eight o'clock about sunset hanging due opposite the house in the east the greatest stack of cloud, to call it one cloud, I ever can recall seeing. Singled by the eye and taken up by itself it was shining white but taken with the sky, which was a strong hard blue, it was anointed with warm brassy glow: only near the earth it was stunned with purplish shadow. The instress of its size came from comparison not with what was visible but with the remembrance of other clouds: like the Monte Rosa range from the Gorner Grat its burliness forced out everything else and loaded the eye-sight. It was in two lines fairly level above and below but not equal in breadth—as 2 to 3 or 3 to 4 perhaps—like two waggons or loaded trucks. The left was rawly made, a fleece parcelled in waving locks flowing open upwards, with shady gutters between, like the ringlets of a ram's fleece blowing; the right was shapely, roped like a heavy cable being slowly paid and by its weight settling into gross coils and beautifully plotted with tortoise-shell squares of shading— indeed much as a snake is plotted, and this one rose steep up like an immeasurable cliff.

In returning the sky in the west was in a great wide-winged or shelved rack of rice-white fine pelleted fretting. At sunset it gathered downwards and as the light then bathed it from below the fine ribbings and long windled jetties dripping with fiery bronze had the look of being smeared by some blade which had a little flattened and richly mulled what it was drawn across. This bronze changed of course to crimson and the whole upper sky being now plotted with pale soaked blue rosettings seized some of it forward in wisps or plucks of smooth beautiful carnation or of coral or camellia rose-colour.

February 23. A lunar halo: I looked at it from the upstairs library window. It was a grave grained sky, the strands rising a little from left to right. The halo was not quite round, for in the first place it was a little pulled and drawn below, by the refraction of the lower air perhaps, but what is more it fell in on the nether left hand side to rhyme the moon itself, which was not quite at full. I could not but strongly feel in my fancy the odd instress of this, the moon leaning on her side, as if fallen back, in the cheerful light floor within the ring, after with magic rightness and success tracing round her the ring the steady copy of her own outline. But this sober grey darkness and pale light was happily broken through by the orange of the pealing of Mitton bells.

Another night from the gallery window I saw a brindled heaven, the moon just masked by a blue spot pushing its way through the darker cloud, underneath and on the skirts of the rack bold long flakes whitened and swaled like feathers, below the garden with the heads of the trees and shrubs furry grey: I read a broad careless inscape flowing throughout.

August 14. Very beautiful sunset; first I think criss-cross yellow flosses, then a graceful level shell of streamers spreading from the sundown. The smoke of the streamers rose lagging in very long-limbed zigzags of flat black vapour, the town was overhung and shadowed by odd minglings of smoke, and the sea at high tide brimming the bay was striped with rose and green like an apple.

July 22. Very hot, though the wind, which was south, dappled very sweetly on one's face and when I came out I seemed to put it on like a gown, as a man puts on the shadow he walks into and hoods or hats himself with the shelter of a roof, a penthouse, or a copse of trees, I mean it rippled and fluttered like light linen, one could feel the folds and braids of it—and indeed a floating flag is like wind visible, and what weeds are in a current; it gives it thew and fires it and bloods it in. Thunderstorm in the evening, first booming in gong-sounds, as at Aosta, as if high up and so not reechoed from the hills; the lightning very slender and nimble and as if playing very near but after supper it was so bright and terrible some people said they had never seen its like. People were killed, but in other parts of the country it was more violent than with us. Flashes lacing two clouds above or the cloud and the earth started upon the eyes in live veins of rincing or riddling liquid white, inched and jagged as if it were the shivering of a bright riband string which had once been kept bound round a blade and danced back into its pleating. Several strong thrills of light followed the flash but a grey smother of darkness blotted the eyes if they had seen the fork, also dull furry thickened scapes of it were left in them.

Bright sunset: all the sky hung with tall tossed clouds, in the west with strong printing glass edges, westward lamping with tipsy buff light, the colour of yellow roses. Partick ridge like a pale goldish skin without body. The plain about Clitheroe was sponged out by a tall white storm of rain. The sun itself and the spot of 'session' dappled with big laps and flowers-in-damask of cloud.

Fine sunset, November 3. Balks of grey cloud searched with long crimsonings running along their hanging folds—this from the lecture room window. A few minutes later the brightness over; one great dull rope coiling overhead sidelong from the sunset, its dewlaps and bellyings painted with a maddery campion-colour that seemed to stoop and drop like sopped cake; the further balk great gutterings and ropings, gilded above, jotted with a more bleeding red beneath and then a juicy tawny 'clear' below, which now is glowing orange and the full moon is rising over the house.

July 23. To Beaumont: it was the Rector's day. It was a

lovely day: shires-long of pearled cloud under cloud, with a
grey stroke underneath marking each row; the beautiful blush-
ing yellow in the straw of the uncut ryefields, the wheat looking
white and all the ears making a delicate and very true crisping
along the top and with just enough air stirring for them to come
and go gently; then there were fields reaping.

September 6. With Wm. Kerr, who took me up a hill behind ours (ours is Mynefyr), a furze-grown and heathy hill, from
which I could look round the whole country, up the valley towards Ruthin and down to the sea. The cleave in which Bod-
fari and Caerwys lie was close below. It was a leaden sky,
braided or roped with cloud, and the earth in dead colours, grave
but distinct. The heights by Snowdon were hidden by the
clouds but not from distance or dimness. The nearer hills, the
other side of the valley, spewed a hard and beautifully detached
and glimmering brim against the light, which was lifting there.
All the length of the valley the skyline of hills was flowingly
written all along upon the sky. A blue bloom, a sort of meal,
seemed to have spread upon the distant south, enclosed by a
basin of hills. Looking all round but most in looking far up the
valley, I felt an instress and charm of Wales.

Afterwards a lovely sunset of rosy juices and creams and
combs; the combs I mean scattered floating vats or rafts or racks
above, the creams, the strew and bed of the sunset, passing
north and south or rather north only into grey material and
brush along the horizon to the hills. Afterwards the rosy field
of the sundown turned gold and the slips and creamings in it
stood out like brands, with jots of purpose. A sodden twilight
over the valley and foreground all below, holding the corner-
hung maroon-grey diamonds of ploughfields to one keeping but
allowing a certain glare in the green of the near tufts of grass.

September 27. At rising I saw a long slender straight river
of dull white cloud rolling down all the bed of the Clwyd from
as far as I could look up the valley to the sea, in height perhaps
twice as high as the Cathedral tower. Its outline rose and fell
regularly in low or shallow eaves or swellings like smooth knots
in a bamboo; and these swellings seemed not to be upwards
only but also to bulge every way, encroaching on the fields as

well. I could also see that it had a flaky or vertebrated make, the flakes leaning forward and curling and falling over a little. St. Asaph with the tower and trees and other spots appeared in grey washes at thinnings or opening of the mist. At that time it was dull but cleared to a lovely day—we have been having indeed a second summer—but in the evening a fog came suddenly on and then cleared again.

It was a fresh and delightful sight. The day was rainy and a rolling wind; parts of the landscape, as the Orms' Heads, were blotted out by rain. The clouds westwards were a pied piece— sail-coloured brown and milky blue; a dun yellow tent of rays opened upon the skyline far off. Cobalt blue was poured on the hills bounding the valley of the Clwyd and far in the south spread a bluish damp, but all the nearer valley was showered with tapered diamonds flakes of fields in purple and brown and green.

July 13. I have seen it [a comet] at bedtime in the west, with head to the ground white, a soft well-shaped tail not big : I felt a certain awe and instress, a feeling of strangeness, flight (it hangs like a shuttlecock at the height before it falls) and of threatening.

November 12, 1883. Yesterday the sky was striped with cirrus cloud like the swaths of a hayfield; only in the east there was a bay or reach of clear blue sky, and in this the shadow-beams appeared, slender, colourless and radiating every way like a fan wide open. To-day the sky was cloudless except for a low bank in the west. In the east was a cast of blue mist from which sprang alternate broad bands of rose colour and blue slightly fringed.

December 16, 1883. A bright glow had been round the sun all day and became more remarkable towards sunset. It then had a silvery or steely look with soft radiating streamers and little colour . . . there was a pale gold colour brightening and fading by turns as the sun went down. After the sunset the horizon was lined a long way by a glowing tawny light, not very pure in colour and distinctly textured in hummocks, bodies like a shoal of dolphins or in what are called gadroons or as the Japanese conventionally represent waves. The glowing vapour above this was as yet colourless; then this took a beautiful olive or celadon green, and delicately fluted; the green belt was broader than the orange and pressed down on and contracted it. Above the green in turn appeared a red glow broader and burlier in make; it was softly brindled and in the ribs or bars of colour was rosier; in the channels where the blue of the sky shone through it was a mallow colour. Above this was a vague lilac . . . the red had driven out the green and fusing with the remains of the orange reached the horizon. By that time the east which had a rose tinge became of a duller red compared to sand; the ground of the sky in the east was green or else tawny and the crimson only in the clouds. A great sheet of heavy dark cloud with a reefed or puckered make drew off the west in the course of the pageant: the edge of this and the smaller pellets of cloud that filed across the bright field of the sundown caught a livid green. The red in the west was fainter because notably rosier and livelier, but it was never of a pure rose. A faint dusky blush was left. While these changes were going on in the sky the landscape of Ribblesdale glowed with a frowning brown.

December 21, 1883. The glow is intense, it has prolonged the daylight and optically changed the season; it bathes the whole sky. It is mistaken for the reflection of a great fire . . . more like inflamed flesh than the lucid reds of ordinary sunsets. But it is also lustreless. A bright sunset lines the cloud so that their brims look like gold, brass, bronze or steel. It fetches out those dazzling flecks and spangles which people call fish scales. It gives to a mackerel or dappled cloud rack the appearance of quilted crimson silk or a ploughed field glazed with crimson ice.

INDEX